Light Intervention

Lessons from Bougainville

Praise for *Light Intervention: Lessons from Bougainville*

"This volume provides an excellent overview of the peacebuilding intervention in Bougainville. Regan demonstrates a deep understanding of the issues at hand, due to his long-standing personal involvement in the Bougainville peacebuilding process. His analysis is profound, his assessments well established, and his recommendations highly original. This book shows what a thorough case study analysis of a specific successful peacebuilding process can contribute to the scholarly and political debate on the problems of international peacebuilding interventions."

—**Volker Boege,** research fellow, University of Queensland

"Few peace processes offer more interesting and neglected lessons than Bougainville. If you read one work to learn them, choose Light Intervention. *Anthony Regan is the preeminent scholar of the Bougainville conflict. His book is a caution against going too far with the view that peacebuilding success depends on intensive multidimensional international intervention and strong state building. It was the humility of New Zealand, the UN, and other internationals that created space for a peace where locals called the shots. Regan documents evocatively how bottom-up local reconciliation with a lot of leadership from women set creative foundations for this peace."*

—**John Braithwaite,** Australian Research Council Federation Fellow and winner of the *Grawemeyer Award for Ideas Improving World Order* and the *Stockholm Prize in Criminology*

"Anthony Regan is without peer in his insightful and erudite understanding of the Bougainville Crisis and the peace process that ended it. This book is important for global peacekeeping. Too often international interventions become part of the problem, not part of the solution. Regan's thesis on Light Intervention *represents a compelling alternative to a burgeoning intervention industry that imposes Western templates and facilitates development dependency. His emphasis on respecting the aspirations and capacities of the host nation's civil society, and its traditional customs and culture is timely."*

—**Bob Breen,** author of *Volume V of the Official History of Peacekeeping, Humanitarian and Post-Cold War Operations, Good Neighbour Operations: Australian Peacemaking and Peacekeeping in the South Pacific 1980–2006*

"The signing of the Bougainville Peace Agreement in 2001 has been generally acknowledged as one of the more successful peace processes of recent decades. Yet the details of the conflict and of the complex negotiations, which culminated in the Peace Agreement, are not well known outside the immediate region. In this volume, the story is carefully unraveled by one of the people who played a significant role in the achievement of a settlement. His authoritative analysis of the emerging conflict, the early failures of government policy, and the eventual movement towards resolution, reconciliation, and rehabilitation—a process characterized by what Regan describes as 'light intervention'—makes a valuable contribution to the literature of internal conflict and conflict resolution. Like all conflicts, that on Bougainville is in some respects unique; but as this volume clearly demonstrates, there are lessons to be learned from the Bougainville experience."

—**Ron May,** The Australian National University

"This is an excellent single case study that presents lessons succinctly and persuasively, with analytical sections that are refreshingly free from jargon. This work on the Bougainville case will be useful to government decision-makers and practitioners, IGOs and NGOs, and academics interested in conflict analysis and resolution, state building and development, and the Asia-Pacific region."

—**Christopher Mitchell,** emeritus professor of conflict research, Institute for Conflict Analysis & Resolution, George Mason University

"This is a story of small details and large conclusions of a small peacemaking effort in a small conflict. We can learn much from it, for big ones too. The twenty-five lessons at the end are deeply pertinent, and the story of the process behind them is good reading too."

—**I. William Zartman,** professor emeritus, Johns Hopkins University-SAIS and editor of *Peacemaking in International Conflict*

Light Intervention

Lessons from Bougainville

Anthony J. Regan

UNITED STATES INSTITUTE OF PEACE PRESS
Washington, DC

The views expressed in this book are those of the authors alone. They do not necessarily reflect views of the United States Institute of Peace.

United States Institute of Peace
1200 17th Street, NW, Suite 200
Washington, DC 20036-3011
www.usip.org

First published 2010.

Printed in the United States of America

The paper used in this publication meets the minimum requirements of American National Standards for Information Science—Permanence of Paper for Printed Library Materials, ANSI Z39.48-1984.

Cartography—GIS Services, The Australian National University, College of Asia and the Pacific

Library of Congress Cataloging-in-Publication Data

Regan, Anthony J.
Light intervention : lessons from Bougainville / Anthony J. Regan.
p. cm.
ISBN 978-1-60127-061-0 (alk. paper)
1. Peace-building—Papua New Guinea—Bougainville Island. 2. Conflict management—Papua New Guinea—Bougainville Island. 3. Intervention (International law). 4. Bougainville Island (Papua New Guinea)—Politics and government. 5. Bougainville Island (Papua New Guinea)—Social conditions. I. Title.
JZ5584.P26R44 2010
995.305—dc22

2010016820

Contents

Abbreviations

ABG	Autonomous Bougainville Government
AusAID	Australian Agency for International Development
BCC	Bougainville Constitutional Commission
BCA	Bougainville Copper Agreement
BCL	Bougainville Copper Ltd
BIG	Bougainville Interim Government
BIPG	Bougainville Interim Provincial Government
BPC	Bougainville People's Congress
BRA	Bougainville Revolutionary Army
BRF	Bougainville Resistance Forces
BTG	Bougainville Transitional Government
BTT	Bougainville Transitional Team
CRA	Conzinc Riotinto Australia Ltd
GIF	Governance and Implementation Fund
JSB	Joint Supervisory Body
MDF	Me'ekamui Defense Force
MGU	Me'ekamui Government of Unity
NSPG	North Solomons Provincial Government
PMG	Peace Monitoring Group
PNG	Papua New Guinea
PNGDF	Papua New Guinea Defense Force
PPCC	Peace Process Consultative Committee
PPSC	Peace Process Steering Committee
SPPKF	South Pacific Peace Keeping Force
TMG	Truce Monitoring Group
UDI	Unilateral Declaration of Independence
UN	United Nations
UNDP	United Nations Development Program
UN-DPA	United Nations Department of Political Affairs
UN-DPKO	United Nations Department of Peace Keeping Operations
UNOMB	United Nations Observer Mission Bougainville
UNPOB	United Nations Political Office Bougainville

Map 1: Bougainville in the Pacific

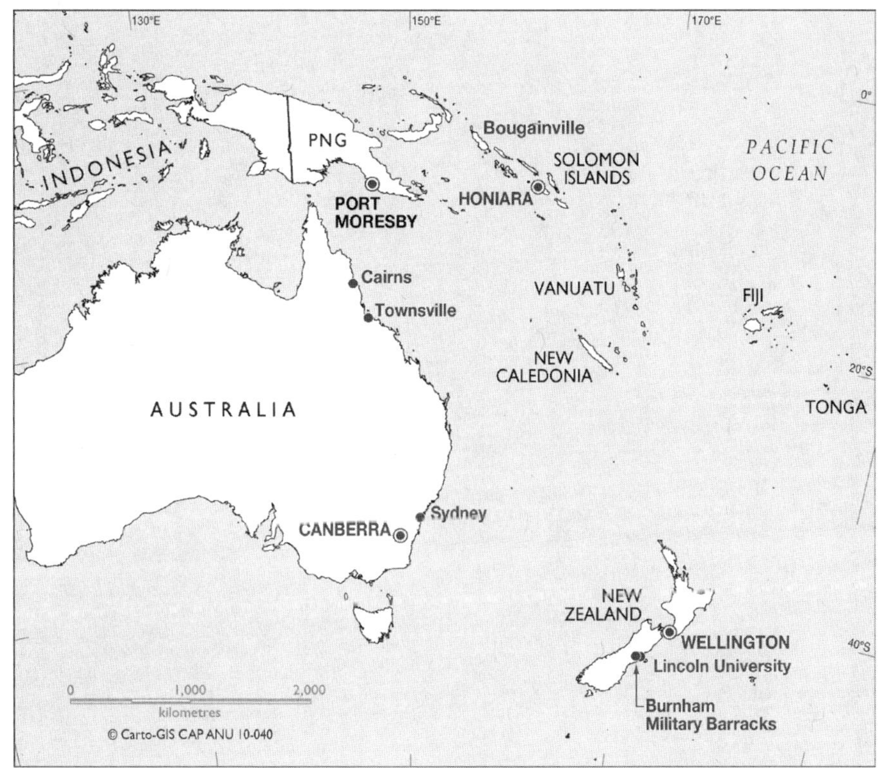

Map 2: Papua New Guinea, Bougainville, and the Solomon Islands

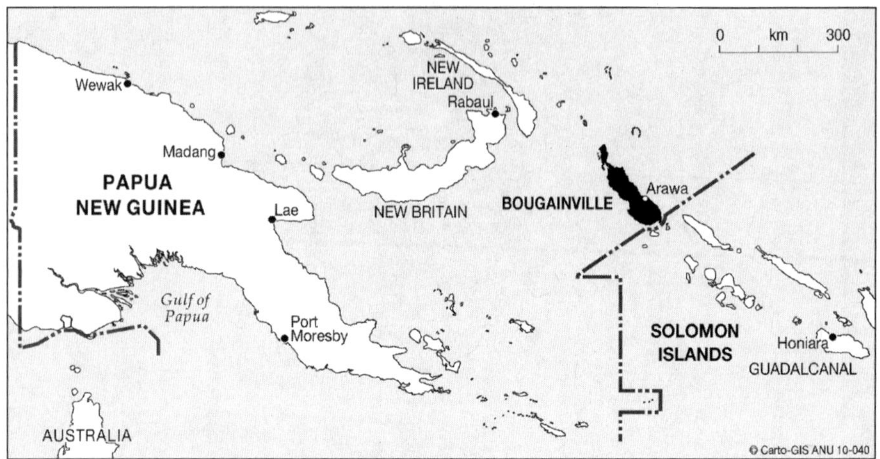

Map 3: The Languages of Bougainville

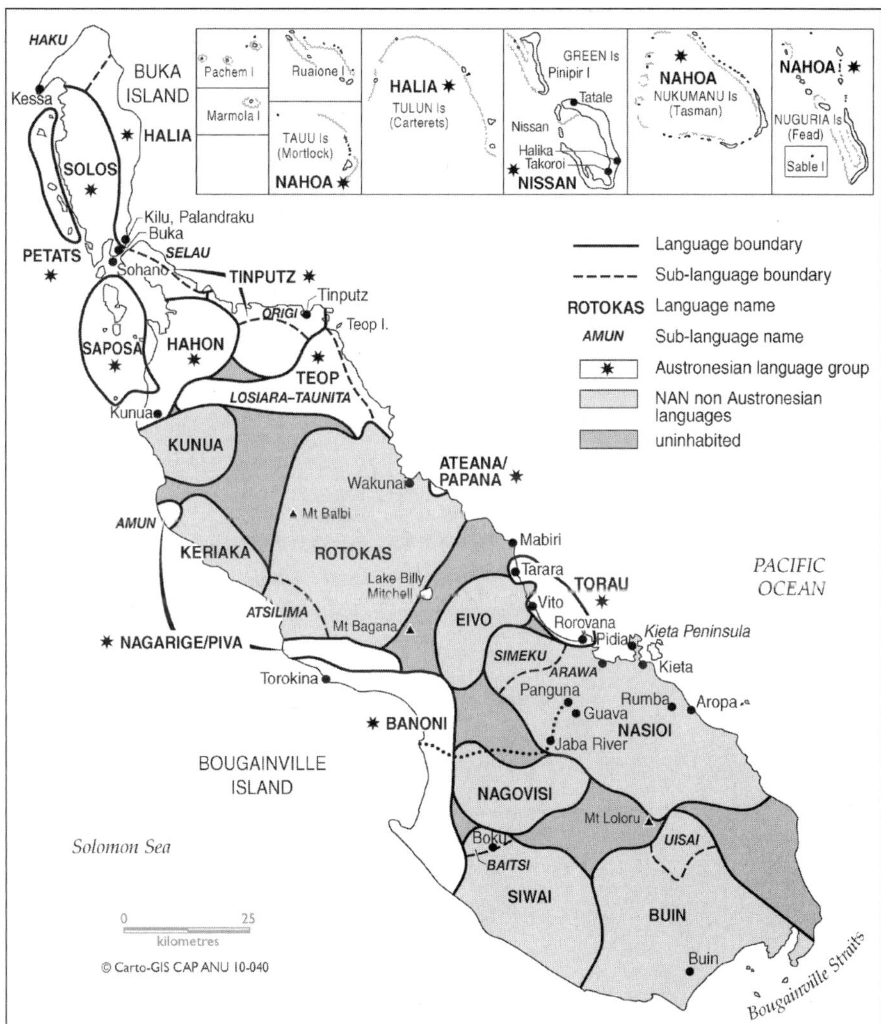

Map 4: Bougainville

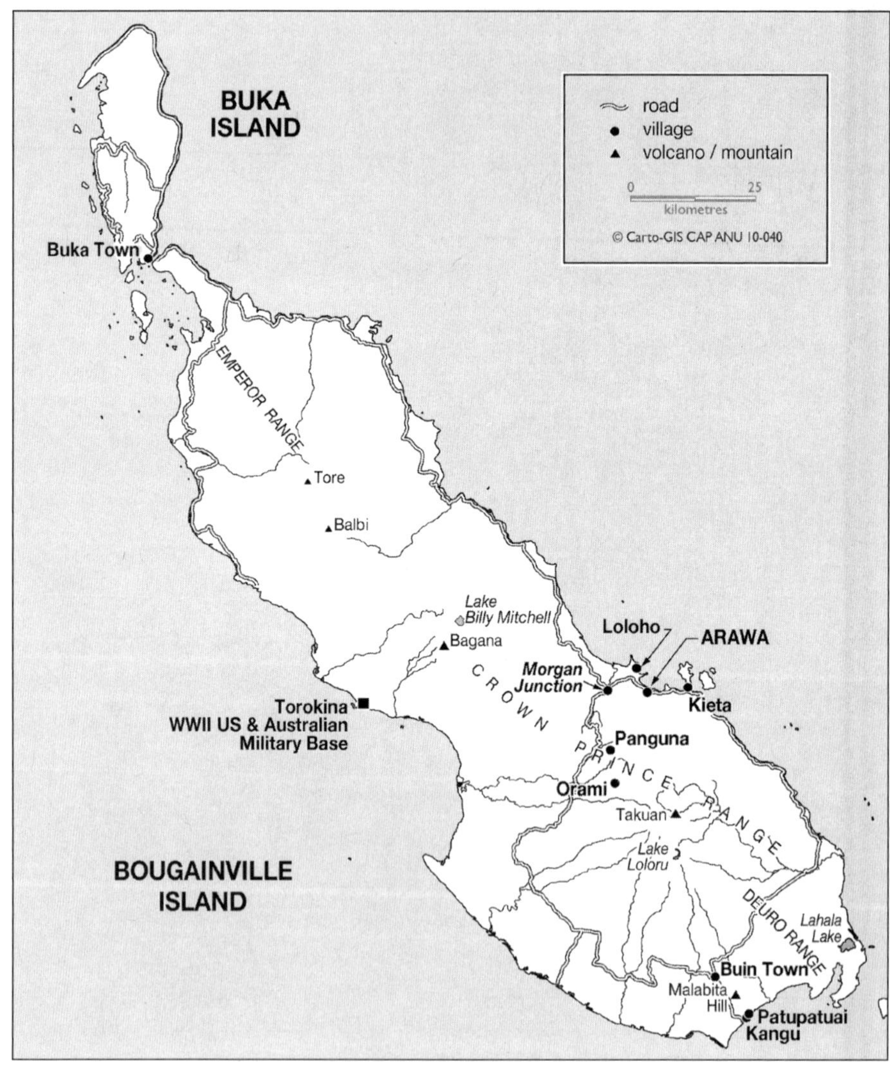

Map 5: BRA Company Areas, 1996–97

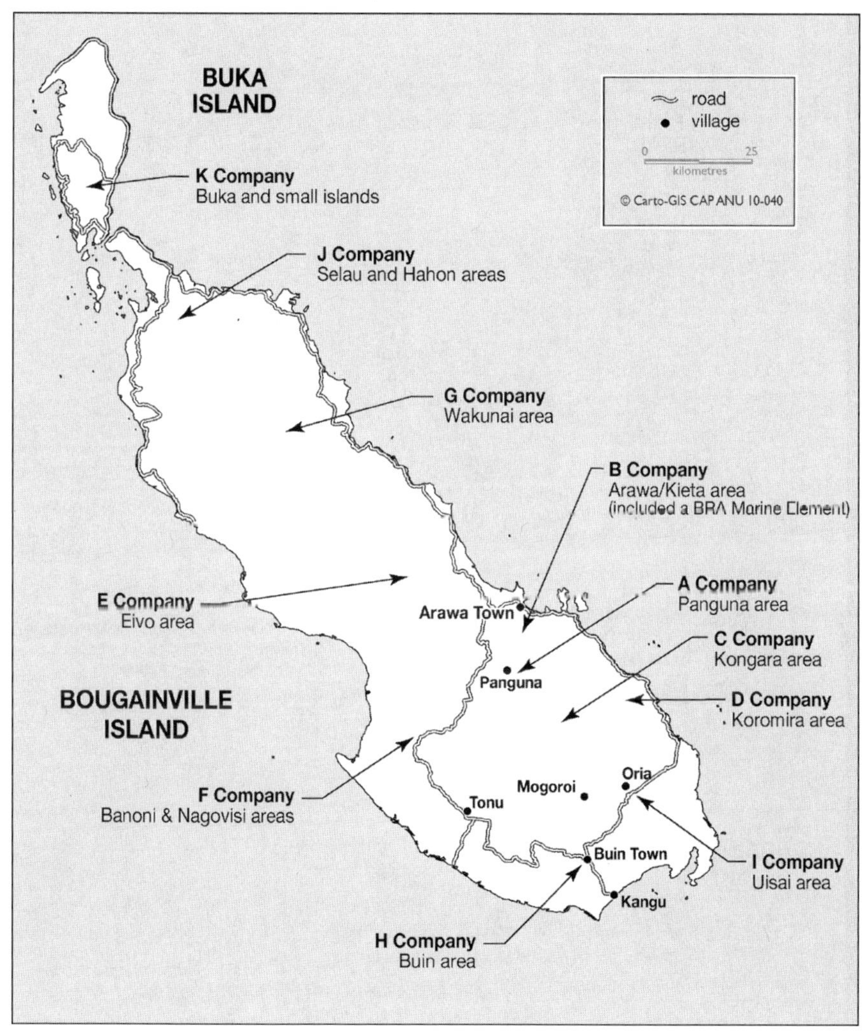

Map 6: Bougainville During the Peace Process, 1997–2010

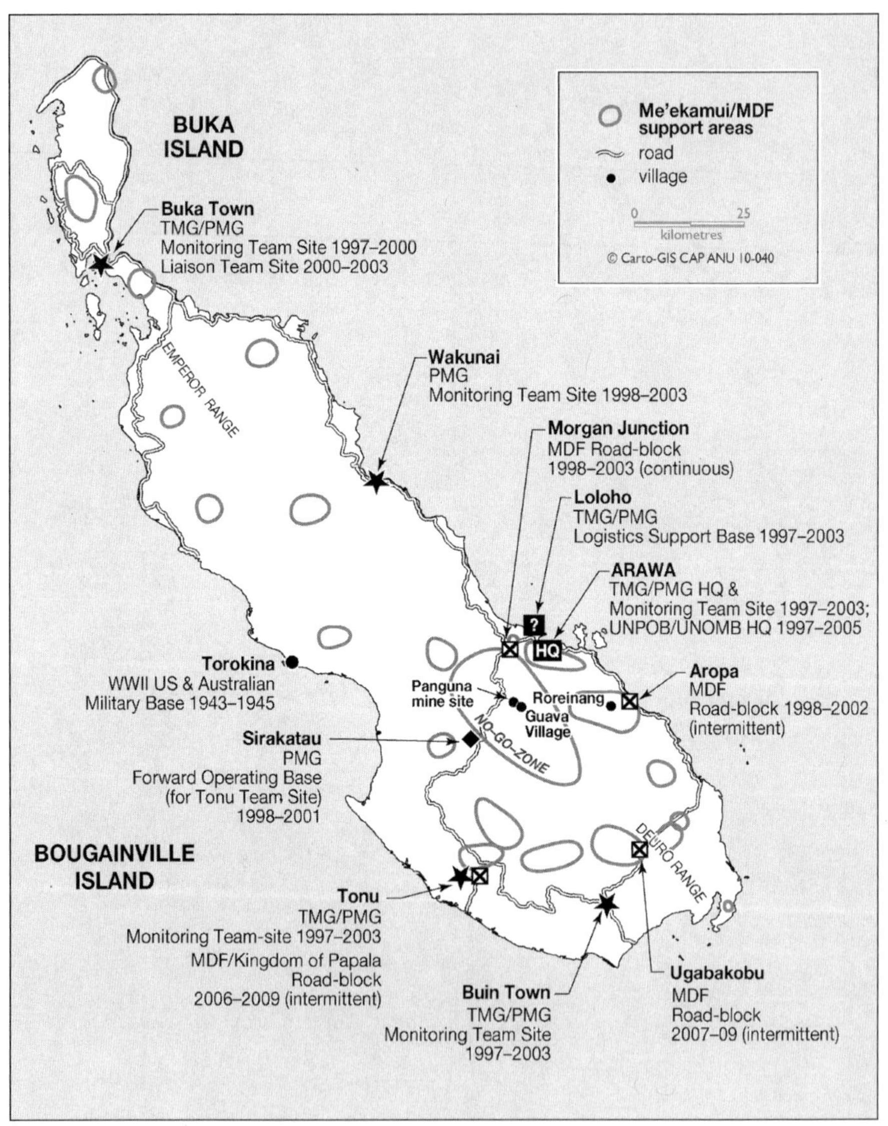

Introduction

The ongoing peace process that began in 1997 in Bougainville, in the southwest Pacific state of Papua New Guinea (PNG), is little known, perhaps because it lacks the geostrategic gravity of many other peace initiatives. It is of particular note, however, for several significant reasons.

First, so far this has been a remarkably successful process, ending (to date) a violent and deeply divisive separatist conflict that for much of the period from 1988 to 1997 destabilized both PNG and the wider Pacific islands region. After many failed peace initiatives that seemed to contribute to more hostility, with conflict intensifying considerably from early 1996, the situation seemed to have become intractable. The success of the process is all the more remarkable given the part played by significant "spoilers," as well as ongoing tensions and local armed conflict that threatened to derail the process at various points—even after the main parties involved in the intervention had departed.

Second, the process related to a multiparty conflict where the adversaries were often nothing more than loose coalitions. Not only was the situation in Bougainville deeply factionalized, but throughout the conflict the PNG government was itself divided and its policies and actions uncoordinated. Such characteristics are increasingly common in intrastate conflict, often giving rise to issues and problems not well addressed by conflict resolution theories derived from relatively simple bilateral conflicts.[1] The Bougainville case highlights some of the difficulties and offers some approaches to actors in interventions faced with similar

1. I am grateful to Chris Mitchell for highlighting the significance of this issue to this study.

I am grateful to Ginny Bouvier and Kurt Volkan for wise counsel and helpful editorial guidance and to Chris Mitchell and an anonymous reviewer for constructive comments on an earlier draft of the paper, all of which much improved this monograph. I am also grateful to Raymond Apthorpe, John Braithwaite, Danielle Brand-Lemond, Bob Breen, David Hallett, Stephen Henningham, Hank Nelson, and John Siau for enlightened comments on earlier drafts.

circumstances (including the particular dangers if armed conflict resumes after intervention).

Third, the process itself was unusual in that it was both initiated and largely controlled by local actors, with the international community playing mainly a supporting and facilitating role.

Fourth, a multifaceted international intervention—mainly a regional "coalition of the willing" and a small United Nations (UN) observer mission—played significant roles in the Bougainville process for an extended period (1997–2005).

Fifth, perhaps the most remarkable aspects of the intervention was the fact that it was, in many ways, the archetypal "light footprint" intervention, which peacebuilding policymakers, practitioners, and students generally acknowledge should be the model pursued by all intervention—one with the lowest possible local impact. Such an intervention is generally regarded as involving the local control and ownership needed for an intervention to be sustainable, helps manage safety risks for those making the intervention, reduces costs and minimizes local dependency, and makes exit strategies manageable.

Sixth, with the benefit of hindsight, the peace process could have benefited from a bit more flexibility with regard to the "weight" of the intervention. While a light footprint intervention tends to focus on the earliest possible exit, more flexibility is required for interventions in such complex multiparty conflicts. For example, a small intervention force that could return when localized armed conflict threatened the peace process might have reduced the serious risks of undermining the long-term process as occurred in Bougainville from late 2005 to early 2010.

The question of why a light footprint intervention was possible in Bougainville is a central focus of this monograph. Policymakers and representatives of international bodies in Washington, D.C.; London; Canberra, and other national capitals increasingly assume an almost countervailing need for both multiple agendas in, and a consequential high degree of international community control of, international peacebuilding interventions. The assumptions seem to be much the same not just situations following intense conflict or when a state collapses, but also more generally where a state is weak. The agenda of activities of the international community in such interventions has expanded in recent years, so much so that it sometimes seems to be assumed that there must be a correct or most productive approach to such activities—perhaps even that templates are available. This agenda—so extensive that it can be quite difficult to achieve a light footprint intervention—generally includes

- provision of a robust peacekeeping (or, if necessary, peace-enforcement) role;
- mediation and other support for achieving a political settlement between opposing combatant and political groups;
- disarmament, demobilization, and reintegration of combatants;
- active engagement in state-building—in relation to both the civil service generally and the law and justice sector in particular, including stepping in to provide these "from scratch" as needed, or rebuilding damaged local capacity through injecting experts and providing capacity-building support to local officials;
- provision of aid and investment packages in support of economic reconstruction;
- development of appropriate postconflict constitutional arrangements, which—in situations where there has been ethnic conflict—often include, among other things, executive and/or territorial power sharing, limits on executive powers, a constitutional court, strong protections for human rights, and a transitional justice mechanism such as a truth and reconciliation process; and
- provision of support for—and/or organization of—elections for a new government.

Of course, while a light footprint is widely regarded as desirable, it is also generally recognized that there are some conflict situations where this cannot be achieved. Further, other factors than those outlined in the extensive agenda of activities could influence the weight of the footprint. A case could vary greatly depending on the local context, changing circumstances, and the particular phase of the intervention in question. For example, in relation to the importance of phases, an initial demonstration of a high level of force might well be justified to encourage particular armed groups to lay down their weapons, but subsequent intervention stages might then be quite limited, or vice versa.

Despite such caveats, the burgeoning scope of the agenda of intervention activities seems to be a major factor leading toward an increasingly heavier footprint. It is in this context that the Bougainville peace process is of particular interest, because while it included most elements of the above agenda, it still managed to achieve a light footprint.

Of course, making comparisons among conflicts, peace processes, and peacebuilding interventions that occur in vastly differing contexts is a task fraught with difficulty. Aspects of the Bougainville situation lent themselves to a far lighter international community involvement than may be necessary in some other cases. Even so, the Bougainville case supports the view that when carrying out peacebuilding interventions, the international community can sometimes achieve more by being less activist than can often seem necessary. Hence, as noted, it serves as a key example when considering both the advantages of, and the conditions that may be necessary for, a light footprint international intervention.

This case study of the Bougainville peace process pays particular attention to the international intervention and its role in the wider peace process. The seven chapters are organized as follows. Chapter 1 presents an overview of facts and issues about the location. Chapter 2 outlines the little-known case of the Bougainville conflict, its origins, main features, and impacts. Chapter 3 provides an overview of the chief facets of the peace process, including some of its main difficulties and the key dynamics that enabled local actors to initiate and largely control it. Chapter 4 turns to the international intervention, focusing on the outside actors involved and their relationships to local actors to explain the significant degree of local control. Chapter 5 deals with the key features of the Bougainville Peace Agreement of August 2001 and the extent of its implementation in the nearly nine years since it was signed. Chapter 6 examines ongoing sources of tension and conflict in Bougainville, with particular attention paid to localized armed conflict in the period since 2005 and, among other things, whether this experience points to shortcomings in the international intervention. Chapter 7 pinpoints some major lessons that the international community might derive from the experience of the Bougainville intervention. Finally, the monograph concludes with key reasons why the international intervention in Bougainville was able to achieve the much sought-after goal of a light footprint.

A Note on the Sequence of Events in Bougainville

The history of Bougainville, of the conflict (both its origins and the course of events 1988–97), and of the peace process is complex. To date there is not yet a single volume that presents even an overview of those events, especially those during the conflict and the peace process. This book does not seek to fill that gap. Further, the analytical approach used here does not present the events of the period 1988 to 2010 in sequence. To assist the reader to better understand the sequence of events, a "Chronology: Main Events in the Bougainville Conflict and Peace Process" is included toward the end of this monograph.

1

Bougainville and Papua New Guinea

Prior to presenting an outline of the origins and main contours of the Bougainville conflict, it is necessary to highlight a few key issues about the geography, history, culture, and economy of both Papua New Guinea, as a whole, and Bougainville, in particular.

Geography, History, and Culture

Bougainville, about 1,000 kilometers east of Port Moresby (PNG's mainland capital city), is the most geographically remote part of the island nation. The largest country of the Pacific islands in terms of both area and population, PNG is one of the most culturally and linguistically diverse countries in the world—its 6 to 7 million people speak more than 850 different languages and incorporate a remarkable range of cultural differences, sometimes even within quite small language groups (especially where parts of such a language group occupy several distinct ecological niches).[1] Map 1 shows PNG in relation to Australia and neighboring countries and territories in the Pacific Ocean, while Map 2 shows Bougainville in relation to the rest of PNG and also the neighboring country of Solomon Islands.

Known as the Autonomous Region of Bougainville since 2005, Bougainville—9,438 square kilometers with approximately 200,000 inhabitants—represents about 2 percent of PNG's total land area and less than four percent of PNG's population. Yet with about 25 of the 850 distinct languages spoken in PNG, as well as many more sublanguages and dialects (see Map 3), Bougainville fits PNG's pattern of linguistic and cultural diversity. There are, however, also many similarities in culture across not just PNG (including Bougainville) but also other countries in what is known as the Melanesian cultural area, which includes Solomon Islands, Vanuatu, and Indonesia's Papua provinces. The most

1. For a discussion of the phenomenon of the impact of ecological niches on cultural differences in the Bougainville context, see Eugene Ogan, "The Cultural Background to the Bougainville Crisis," *Journal de la Société des Océanistes*, vols. 92–93 (1992), 61–67.

significant physical distinction between Bougainvilleans and people elsewhere in PNG is the very dark skin color of most (but not all) Bougainvilleans.[2]

Bougainville (see Map 4) consists of the large island of Bougainville, the smaller but densely populated island of Buka (separated from Bougainville Island by a narrow sea passage), and many smaller islands. Geographically, culturally, and linguistically, Bougainville is the northernmost part of the Solomon Islands chain. It became part of PNG rather than Solomon Islands (a British colonial possession until 1978) through "accidents" of late-nineteenth-century colonial map makers. It was in 1886 that Bougainville was legally incorporated into German New Guinea, which was made up mainly of the northern portion of the eastern half of the large island of New Guinea together with various islands to its north and east, inclusive of Bougainville.

The first humans arrived in Bougainville from the north about 30,000 years ago, and linguists and pre-historians generally agree that they did not speak Austronesian languages; descendants of these early arrivals are now located in the central and southern parts of the main island of Bougainville (see Map 3). There was a further wave of migration from the north about 3,000 to 4,000 years ago, and it is generally agreed that these peoples spoke Austronesian languages, which continue to be used mainly in Buka and the north of Bougainville Island (Map 3). Apart from these two waves of human settlement, Bougainville remained largely isolated from the rest of the world until the first European explorers arrived there in the late eighteenth century.[3] Until then Bougainvilleans comprised small stateless societies—not even the 25 language groups constituted political units, and there was considerable cultural diversity even within the larger language groups. Small clan-based, land-holding groups, usually of just 50 to 200 people, were the main social units.

2. For a discussion of the reasons for the dark skin color of most Bougainvilleans (something unique in the Pacific islands region), see Jonathan Friedlander, "Why Do the People of Bougainville Look Unique?" in Anthony Regan and Helga Griffin, eds., *Bougainville before the Conflict* (Canberra: Pandanus Press, 2005), 57–70.

3. For an overview of Bougainville's prehistory, see Matthew Spriggs, "Bougainville's Early History: An Archaeological Perspective," in Regan and Griffin, *Bougainville before the Conflict*, 1–19.

Colonial control over Bougainville and its integration into PNG are quite recent. Although legally under German control since 1886, and used as a source of labor for German plantations and the colonial police force elsewhere in German New Guinea, the first permanent Christian mission and colonial administrative post (under German New Guinea) was not established until 1901 (in Buin, in south Bougainville) and 1905 (at Kieta, on the east coast in central Bougainville), respectively (see Map 4). In its first brief period under direct colonialism, Bougainville was a remote and very lightly administered part of German New Guinea. The colonial administration had few permanent posts and mounted limited patrols mainly in coastal areas and accessible plains. Copra and cocoa plantations were established in some parts of the east and northwest coasts of Bougainville Island. European Catholic missionaries established stations mainly in coastal areas. German administration ended in 1914 when Australian forces took control of German New Guinea at the beginning of World War I. From 1921 Australia was granted a League of Nations mandate over former German New Guinea, and Bougainville then became a remote area in the Australian territory of New Guinea. There was limited colonial government activity between the wars, and economic development was largely limited to the expropriated former German plantations. Many young Bougainvillean men worked on plantations both in Bougainville and in other parts of New Guinea. Most people, however, relied largely on subsistence agriculture. Catholic missions (inclusive of schools and health services) expanded under the Australian administration (which left provision of most services to the churches), although from 1917 Catholic missions competed with the Methodist and from 1924 with the Seventh-Day Adventist churches. By World War II, most Bougainvilleans had had some contact with Europeans, except those who lived in some remote mountainous areas.

Bougainville was the site of a significant earlier conflict—namely during World War II.[4] In 1942 the area, then with a population of about 50,000, was occupied by some 65,000 Japanese troops. As part of an island-hopping strategy that had begun with the battle for Guadalcanal

4. For a discussion of the impact of World War II on Bougainville, see Hank Nelson "Bougainville in World War II," in Regan and Griffin, eds., *Bougainville before the Conflict*, 168–98.

(Solomon Islands) (see Map 2) early in 1943, United States Marines (later augmented by U.S. Army forces) landed at Torokina on the west coast of Bougainville despite strong opposition from Japanese troops. Not interested in capturing the rest of Bougainville from the Japanese, the U.S. divisions limited themselves to establishing a huge base and housing 65,000 personnel and three airfields to fly bombing missions against Japanese positions further north in the Pacific. Australian forces took over from the United States at Torokina late in 1944, using it as their base for a campaign to recapture Bougainville from the Japanese. Weapons, ammunition, and explosives abandoned in the area by these forces became a significant source of armaments for Bougainville combatant groups during the conflict from 1988 to 1997 and have also played a part in localized armed conflict from 2005 to 2010.

Following World War II Bougainville was again administered by Australia, this time as part of the United Nations Trust Territory of New Guinea, which for administrative purposes Australia amalgamated with its colonial territory of Papua (the southern part of the eastern half of the island of New Guinea). Bougainville remained a remote part of Australia's territory of Papua and New Guinea. Foreign-owned plantations continued to be the backbone of the commercial economy. The colonial government increasingly promoted small-scale agricultural development from the 1950s and 1960s. As a result, although most Bougainvilleans continued to rely heavily on subsistence agriculture, many also came to derive a cash income from small-scale cultivation of cash crops, especially copra and cocoa, a development that by the 1970s was contributing to not only cash incomes for many, but also land pressures and growing economic inequality. From the 1950s Bougainvilleans generally ceased working as plantation laborers either locally or elsewhere in PNG, forcing the owners of plantations in Bougainville to bring in people from elsewhere in PNG—there were up to 10,000 such outside laborers in the years immediately before the Bougainville conflict. As they finished their contract periods, many tended to stay on in Bougainville, seeking employment and often settling illegally, as squatters, on land belonging to Bougainvilleans. The presence of so many outsiders was a concern to native inhabitants.

Aspects of Bougainville Culture and Identity

Despite the significant impacts of the colonial government, Christian missions, and the plantation economy on Bougainville's social groups and associated cultures, many aspects of its precolonial social and political structures and norms have proved remarkably resilient. Apart from a small proportion of land "alienated" by processes of government or private acquisition (mainly for plantations, Christian missions, and towns), all other land is recognized by the state as owned by clan-based units under longstanding indigenous practices and norms that vary considerably between language and culture groups. They are part of a much broader set of practices and norms that regulate precolonial social and political structures and relations within and among social groups, which are generally referred to in PNG and Bougainville as part of "custom," or "customary ways," which is recognized for many purposes by the PNG constitution and laws. Indeed, under the PNG constitution, "custom" is given a status in law similar to that of the common law in the United States, the United Kingdom, Australia, or New Zealand.

Unusually in Melanesia, most language and culture groups in Bougainville are matrilineal, meaning that descent from the female line dictates the inheritance of land and other property and is a key principle of social organization. While women in Bougainville's matrilineal societies enjoy relatively high status compared to women in not only most of the limited number of matrilineal societies elsewhere in PNG, but also the patrilineal societies that predominate elsewhere in PNG, men still tend to dominate Bougainville's public and political life. Indeed, Bougainville's matrilineal societies might be described as matrilineal in social structures but patriarchal in terms of distribution of power.

In common with patterns elsewhere in PNG and Melanesia, an individual Bougainvillean tends to identify most strongly with a relatively small clan-based family group (comprising a few closely related extended families that together constitute a corporate clan-based, landholding lineage) and with other pervasive localized identity groups. While the larger Bougainvillean language groups, some of perhaps 30,000 people or more, do constitute identity groups for certain purposes, there are also numerous geographically based identity groups within them. Since the advent of colonial contact, long-established patterns of identity formation from precolonial times have been overlaid by a range of new identities emerging in response to colonial and postcolonial social, economic, and political change. These various identities have overlapped and interacted in shifting patterns of generally very localized alliances, tensions, and conflict before, during, and since the period of violent conflict, 1988–97.[5]

While there are hereditary chiefs in some areas (mainly in Buka, as well as in the far north and far south of Bougainville Island), most are chiefs of small groups and have circumscribed powers. Elsewhere, while there may often be a hereditary element to achieving leadership (for example, the eldest male of the main family of a dominant landowning lineage could be expected to be a major leadership figure), leadership tends to be performance based and spread among various people who exercise leadership in relation to different aspects of the social life of the group. In general, neither chiefs nor other leaders can dominate readily—rather, decisions tend to be made by consensus of views among adults, and the mark of a strong leader tends to be the extent of his or her ability to encourage consensus.

Before colonial rule nothing similar to state entities provided Bougainville societies with social stability and order. Rather, the small social groups maintained order on the basis of the balanced reciprocity required for social interaction. Reciprocity was constantly reinforced by ceremonial and other forms of exchange. This pattern of governance has continued into the twenty-first century, although some modification has resulted from colonial rule and Christian missions. Chapter 3 discusses in more detail how the armed conflict from 1988 to 1997 upset this delicate social balance and why understanding the dynamics of local governance was significant during the peace process.

Since engaging with outsiders from the late nineteenth century into the twentieth, Bougainvilleans have developed a common identity that almost certainly did not exist before then. This sense of common identity was distinct from other populations residing in PNG. Bougainvilleans' common dark skin color became the primary marker of this new

5. For a discussion of intra-Bougainville identity issues, see Anthony J. Regan, "Identities among Bougainvilleans," in Regan and Griffin, eds., *Bougainville before the Conflict*, 418–46.

identity, differentiating them from lighter skinned people elsewhere in PNG, whom Bougainvilleans often refer to (pejoratively) as "red-skins." It was only from about the 1950s, however, that identity politics developed in Bougainville. It was initially centered on grievances about colonial neglect.

Mining and the Politicization of Bougainville Identity

Exploration and exploitation of mineral resources on a massive scale in the 1960s led to the politicization of identity as the defining issue in Bougainville's political economy. The presence of a large quantity of low-grade ore body was established in 1964 at Panguna in what had until then been inaccessible mountains in central Bougainville (see Map 4). Exploration and development proceeded rapidly, despite strong opposition from local landowners. Large-scale, open-cut mining began in 1972. It brought rapid economic and social change on a scale not previously imaginable to most Bougainvilleans. The giant Australian mining company, Conzinc Riotinto Australia Ltd (CRA), through its majority-owned subsidiary, Bougainville Copper Ltd (BCL), moved in to operate one of the world's largest copper and gold mines. The administrative capital of Bougainville was moved from Buka Town to Arawa on the east coast, about 25 kilometers from Panguna (see Map 4). The new capital became the center for extensive economic development in the mountains and on the coast where there had been little before. Thousands of people from elsewhere in PNG and from other countries traveled to Bougainville to work for or take advantage of economic opportunities associated with the mine. The presence of so many "white-skins" and "red-skins," additional to the thousands of plantation laborers, was generally resented by many Bougainvilleans, who blamed the outsiders for an increase in crime and other social problems, including the undermining of customary ways. Increasing intermarriage of Bougainvilleans with outsiders caused concern about the long-term future of Bougainvillean identity.

The mine itself was especially resented. It had been established without consulting Bougainville leadership (in fact, no political body capable of representing Bougainvilleans existed until the early 1970s) and against the clear wishes of the landowners whose land was either destroyed in the process of mining or used for purposes associated with mining. Very little compensation was paid to those landowners, in large part because PNG law in both the colonial and postcolonial periods has treated subsurface minerals as the property of the state, a legal view very much at odds with Bougainvilleans' own about land, as reflected in their own customary practices and norms in relation to land. Further, the mine was seen as benefiting the rest of PNG, but leaving Bougainvilleans to bear the high environmental and social costs with little reward beyond the limited rents and compensation paid to landowners in the mine lease areas and the supposed "trickle down" effect on the Bougainville economy. From total earnings of PGK4.4 billion, the mine generated PGK1.754 billion in total profits in its 17 years of operation. Almost one-third went to BCL's parent company (CRA) and shareholders outside PNG, and more than two-thirds to interests in PNG (shareholders including the PNG government, which held a 20 percent stake, as well as in the form of taxes payable to PNG—more than half of that total two-thirds going to the PNG government).[6] Bougainville interests (its provincial government and mine lease landowners) received only a 5.63 percent share—4.27 percent to Bougainville's provincial government (mostly royalties) and 1.36 percent to the owners of land leased by BCL, through a small share of royalties, together with rents and compensation.[7] This distribution of revenue, derived from what they saw as their resources, was deeply resented by both mine-lease landowners and the broader Bougainville leadership. In addition, economic change associated with the mine exacerbated economic inequality among Bougainvilleans and contributed to wider social change, undermining customary authority and ways and contributing to growing concern among Bougainvilleans about wider patterns

6. Paul Quodling, *Bougainville: The Mine and the People* (Sydney: Centre for Independent Studies, 1991), 34. The average exchange rate for the PNG currency, the PGK (kina), against the U.S. dollar over the period in question was around US$1.1.

7. James Griffin and Melchior Togolo, "North Solomons Province, 1974–1990," in May and Regan, *Political Decentralisation in a New State: The Experience of Papua New Guinea* (Bathurst: Crawford House Press, 1997), 354–85, 357, and John Connell, "Compensation and Conflict: The Struggle for Development at the Bougainville Copper Mine," in John Connell and Richard Howitt, eds., *Mining and Indigenous Peoples in Australasia* (Sydney: Sydney University Press, 1991), 55–75.

of economic development over which they had little control and which they tended to blame on the mine.

As resentment about the mine and the outsiders grew in the turbulent politics of the years leading to PNG's independence in 1975, there was increasing talk of secession of Bougainville from PNG as the solution. Educated Bougainvillean leaders interested mainly in achieving some political autonomy for Bougainville, an increased share of mine revenue, and increased economic opportunities for the Bougainville elite mobilized political support through secessionist rhetoric. Disputes about autonomy for Bougainville and its limited share of mining revenue resulted in Bougainville leaders attempting secession through a unilateral declaration of independence (UDI) in September 1975, days before PNG itself achieved independence. By mid-1976, unable to gain any international recognition for a separatist agenda, and facing a PNG government determined to be moderate and conciliatory, Bougainville's leaders agreed to a compromise under which PNG would establish a constitutionally entrenched system of autonomous provincial governments throughout the island nation, a compromise very much in line with the demands Bougainville had been making in the lead-up to PNG independence. Under the agreement, the provincial government for Bougainville received the mining royalties previously payable to the PNG government.[8] While the immediate conflict was resolved, many Bougainvilleans still saw secession as a realistic solution to a wide range of problems, with many believing that the educated leadership of the mid-1970s had been too quick to compromise on the issue.

8. See Yash Ghai and Anthony Regan, *The Law, Politics, and Administration of Decentralisation in Papua New Guinea* (Waigani: PNG National Research Institute, 1992); R. J. May and A. J. Regan, eds., *Political Decentralisation in a New State: The Experience of Papua New Guinea* (Bathurst: Crawford House Press, 1997); Griffin and Togolo, "North Solomons Province."

2

The Bougainville Conflict, 1988 to 1997—An Overview

The complex origins and unfolding of the nine-year conflict have been discussed elsewhere.[1] In brief, the violent conflict that emerged quite unexpectedly beginning in late 1988 was not initially related to secessionist demands, but rather to mining-related concerns, largely involving revenue shares and mine employment opportunities for Bougainvilleans. The violence would probably never have developed into a wider separatist conflict but for the way PNG police mobile squads responded in the early stages of the violence.

Origins of the Conflict

The conflict was precipitated primarily by a combination of three chief sets of grievances and concerns on the part of two main groups of Bougainvilleans—namely owners of customarily owned land (hereafter,

1. See Ronald J. May and Matthew Spriggs, eds., *The Bougainville Crisis* (Bathurst: Crawford House Press, 1990); Douglas Oliver, *Black Islanders: A Personal Perspective of Bougainville, 1937–1991* (Melbourne: Hyland House, 1991); Connell, "Compensation and Conflict"; Matthew Spriggs and Donald Denoon, eds., *The Bougainville Crisis: 1991 Update* (Canberra: Australian National University in association with Crawford House Press, 1992); Terrence Wesley-Smith, ed., "A Legacy of Development: Three Years of Crisis in Bougainville," *Journal of the Contemporary Pacific*, vol. 4, no. 2, special issue (1992); Ogan, "The Cultural Background"; Griffin and Togolo, "North Solomons Province"; Anthony J. Regan, "Causes and Course of the Bougainville Conflict," *Journal of Pacific History*, vol. 33, no. 3 (1998), 269–85; Anthony J. Regan, "Why a Neutral Peace Monitoring Force? The Bougainville Conflict and the Peace Process" and "Establishing the Truce Monitoring Group and the Peace Monitoring Group," both in Monica Wehner and Donald Denoon, eds. *Without a Gun: Australia's Experience of Monitoring Peace in Bougainville, 1997–2001* (Canberra: Pandanus Books, 2001), 1–18, 21–41; Anthony J. Regan, "Bougainville: Beyond Survival," *Cultural Survival Quarterly*, vol. 26, no. 3 (2002), 20–24; Anthony J. Regan, "The Bougainville Conflict: Political and Economic Agendas," in Karen Ballentine and Jake Sherman, eds. *The Political Economy of Armed Conflict: Beyond Greed & Grievance* (Boulder, Colo.: Lynne Rienner, 2003), 133–66; Regan and Griffin, eds., *Bougainville before the Conflict;* Anthony J. Regan, "Development and Conflict in Bougainville," in Anne Brown, ed., *Security and Development in the Pacific Islands: Social Resilience in Emerging States* (Boulder, Colo.: Lynne Rienner, 2007), 89–110.

mine-lease landowners) leased to BCL under the PNG mining statute and young Bougainvillean mine workers. One set of grievances involved internal disputes among the mine-lease landowners, some concerning the share of mine rents and revenue received by younger mine-lease landowners. A second involved grievances of young Bougainvillean employees of BCL about limited recognition of what they saw as the rights of Bougainvilleans to preferential employment treatment—of particular concern was that Bougainvilleans constituted only about one-quarter of BCL's workforce of over 3,000, and many of these employees felt that they were not given sufficient promotion and other advantages. A third involved longstanding concerns among mine-lease landowners and other Bougainvilleans about the environmental and social impacts of the mine, concerns that for some were a basis for seeking a far greater share of mine revenue for Bougainville; others felt that permanent closure of the mine was the only answer.[2]

Facets of Bougainville culture and social structures help to explain the intensity of feeling toward all of these issues. For example, the disputes among landowner groups over distribution of revenue originated in two significant factors.[3] One was the failure in the late 1960s of colonial government officials, when they demarcated landownership arrangements in the mine-lease area, to give sufficient weight to the corporate clan lineages that owned (under customary norms) most of the more than 800 mainly small blocks of land that together comprised the mine lease areas (a minority of blocks were held, under customary principles, by family groups). Instead, they had designated a single member of each clan lineage (or family group) as the "title-holder" of each of the blocks. This contributed to many tensions and disputes within and among landowning lineages about the way these title-holders distributed the rent and compensation monies that they received on behalf of the lineage.[4] A second factor involved failure to make adequate provision to increase

2. The background and key ideas of one influential leader who held such views (Damien Dameng) is discussed in Regan, "Bougainville: Beyond Survival."

3. See Connell, "Compensation and Conflict"; Regan, "The Bougainville Conflict: Political and Economic Agendas"; Regan, "Development and Conflict."

4. For more discussion of issues concerning land demarcation, see Regan, "The Bougainville Conflict: Political and Economic Agendas"; and Regan, "Development and Conflict."

rent and compensation amounts to take account of population growth. By the mid-1980s, increasing numbers of adult members of such lineages felt they had claims on rental and compensation payments from the limited funding pools that were seldom adjusted. In general, younger persons who had become adults in the years after the mine began operating received less than persons who had already been adults in the early 1970s. The younger landowners were resentful, contributing to a significant generational split in leadership, which in the mid-1980s saw a new mine-lease landowners association challenge the leadership of the first mine-lease landowners association that had been established in 1978. Francis Ona, who was also a member of the young Bougainville mine workers, emerged as a key leader of this new association and was soon to be the main leader of a separatist uprising.

In relation to the concerns about not only environmental and social impacts, but also the need for preferential employment treatment, Bougainvilleans generally share a belief that the clan group in any area regarded traditionally as the original occupiers or owners should be accorded special respect. Through the 1970s and 1980s there was growing discussion among Bougainvillean mine employees and groups in the vicinity of the mine that mine-lease landowners and Bougainvilleans more generally should be recognized as the equivalent of original owners and accorded special treatment and special respect by both BCL and the national government. By the time the conflict erupted, however, the concerns of the Bougainvillean mine workers had never even been stated in a set of demands put to BCL—rather, the young mine workers regarded themselves as sharing many of the same grievances as the mine-lease landowners and expected that their shared grievances would be dealt with together.

From the mid-1980s a loose coalition developed between some younger members of mine-lease area landowners groups and young Bougainville mine workers. Several young mine workers, such as Francis Ona, were members of both groups and soon emerged as the leading voices to express commonly shared grievances in the wake of frustration over earlier failed efforts with BCL. In the end, all grievances were eventually combined into one main demand for a huge compensation payment from BCL. The depth of feeling among these young Bougainvilleans and the frustration over previous failures were not understood by either the PNG government or BCL. The tipping point came in November 1988 when a group of young Bougainvillean mine workers led by Ona destroyed power lines essential to the operation of the mine. At this point secession did not figure in the goals of these perpetrators, who were acting mainly to draw attention to concerns related to demands for an increase in the share of mine revenues and the entitlements of Bougainvillean mine workers and mine-lease landowners.

The Conflict Grows and Reaches a Crisis Point

The rapidly escalating destruction of mine property drew a widespread and violent response from PNG police mobile squads, made up almost entirely of those who were not native Bougainvilleans—the so-called red-skins. From early 1989 violent conflict escalated quickly, though mainly in the mine-lease areas and adjacent parts of central Bougainville. Attacks on the mine and its employees resulted in its closure in May 1989, and it has not reopened since, although an estimated 20 years of resources remained.

The police mobile squads often responded with the same indiscriminately brutal behavior against villagers that they were trained to use against tribal fighting elsewhere in PNG. It was this behavior that was the catalyst for mobilization of a wider secessionist rebellion. In a meeting at Orami Village in central Bougainville (see Map 4) with leaders from groups from other parts of Bougainville (outside the mining area) in February 1989, Ona was promised their support if he made Bougainville secession a key goal. Some among this wider support group envisaged both secession and closure of the mine, but Ona and many of the leaders from other parts of Bougainville envisioned the mine reopening once the conflict was over, at which point it would provide the revenue needed to make an independent Bougainville viable.

By mid-1989 the armed groups supporting Francis Ona were generally known as the Bougainville Revolutionary Army (BRA), branches of which were being established in most parts of Bougainville. It was the young Bougainvillean mine workers who had been involved in or supported the destruction of BCL powerlines and other property who provided much of the local BRA leadership when they returned to their home areas in all parts of Bougainville when the mine closed in May 1989. Their agreed strategy was to link with criminal gangs in their home areas as the social elements most likely to have access to and readiness to use weapons as part of conflict with the PNG forces. As that conflict escalated and responses of the PNG forces became ever more brutal, some Bougainvilleans who had previously been members of the Papua New Guinea Defense Force (PNGDF) also joined the BRA, as did other young Bougainvilleans. Under Francis Ona as political leader and Sam Kauona (a PNGDF junior officer who went AWOL early in 1989 in order to assist Ona) as military leader, the BRA developed a loose structure of locally based units, usually with strong links to the communities in which they continued to be based. Map 5 indicates the areas covered by what came to be known as the main BRA companies toward the end of the conflict (around 1996–97). As the locally based BRA groups became established in 1989, they destroyed government property and BCL and other private sector property, and used guerrilla tactics against the police and the PNGDF.

In April 1989 the PNGDF was mobilized for the first time in PNG history to fight citizens. Despite initially being far more disciplined than the police mobile squads and able to deploy much more firepower, the PNGDF (whose members, like the mobile squads, were mainly from elsewhere in PNG) became even more brutal in its treatment of civilians and villages suspected of supporting the BRA as units took on casualties. Of course, such responses only consolidated community support and the flow of recruits to the BRA. For its part, the BRA used threats and violence against Bougainville residents whose origin was elsewhere in PNG. As a result, most such people fled Bougainville during 1989 and early 1990, a form of ethnic cleansing widely welcomed by Bougainvilleans.

From late 1989 the military situation turned decisively against the PNG forces. In March 1990 a ceasefire, witnessed by foreign observers, led the PNGDF to withdraw in conjunction with a "laying down of arms" by the BRA. This withdrawal was to be followed by negotiations about the way forward, with PNG police personnel (70 mobile squad members as well as all general duties police officers stationed in Bougainville) to remain to provide a PNG government presence. But while the PNGDF withdrew as agreed, BRA members merely ceremonially laid down their weapons momentarily and then took them up again. Further, contrary to both the ceasefire agreement and the decision of the PNG cabinet, the police commissioner (who had been in overall command of operations by PNG forces in Bougainville) withdrew the police, apparently in "frustration over the constraints imposed by the government upon the actions of the forces, including the final withdrawal, and the resulting humiliation of himself."[5]

The BRA unexpectedly found itself in control of Bougainville and was initially not sure what to do. The PNG government was equally uncertain, with a moderate prime minister seeking negotiations, while his hard-line deputy prime minister (a former PNGDF commander) was in favor of forcing the BRA to submit by blockading Bougainville. On May 2, 1990, with the prime minister absent from the country, the deputy acted to impose a sea and air blockade of Bougainville, which continued to apply to areas of Bougainville that were not under PNG control until the mid-1990s. It brought great hardship to many Bougainvilleans, especially in terms of loss of access to government health and education services.[6] Meanwhile, on May 17 Francis Ona unilaterally declared Bougainville independent of PNG. Although this was never recognized by any other country, Ona was to continue to assert that his UDI (Unilateral Declaration of Independence) was effective in making Bougainville independent until he died in July 2005, eight years after the peace process had begun. In addition to the UDI, he also established an appointed civilian government—the Bougainville Interim Government (BIG)—in mid-1990.

Even in the early stages of the conflict, support for the BRA was not uniform. There was some opposition to secession, and at the very least ambivalence toward the BRA, especially among coastal communities of Buka and parts of the eastern coast of Bougainville Island. These were areas that, compared to the communities of the sparsely settled north-

5. Oliver, *Black Islanders*, 235–36. See also Graeme Kemmelfield, "A Short History of the Ceasefire Negotiations," in May and Spriggs, *The Bougainville Crisis*, 62–72.

6. The events just outlined are described in more detail by Oliver, *Black Islanders*, 235–45.

west coast and the mountains (including those around the mine site), had a history of more links with the outside world and populations with more formal education and whose leaders recognized the economic and other advantages of some integration into PNG. Further, the BRA was not a monolithic and disciplined organization, but rather involved loosely linked groups based mainly in local communities, with varying degrees of commitment to BRA and BIG ideological goals.

From at least the time when the PNG forces withdrew from Bougainville (March 1990), some BRA elements became embroiled in local conflicts related to old grudges, inequality in wealth, local land disputes, and so on. Other groups had been criminal gangs before the conflict, and once the PNG forces withdrew they reverted to their old ways. The BRA and BIG leadership were unable to control the localized BRA elements, and a semi-anarchic situation developed in many parts of Bougainville, especially (but not only) in urban centers.[7] Not surprisingly, broader, though still mainly localized, intra-Bougainville conflict soon developed in many areas, often related to localized patterns of relations between quite small groups with origins from well before the conflict. Government employees and other Bougainvilleans regarded as sympathetic to PNG were targeted, often a very divisive tactic as such people usually had high standing in their own communities. Gradually there were increasing numbers of armed clashes involving opposing BRA elements. By mid-1990 some communities were suffering directly from localized conflict or were feeling under intense threat. It was chiefs and other community leaders from the north of Buka who first sought assistance from the PNG security forces; as a result, the PNGDF made a forced landing in the Buka Town (see Map 4) in September 1990 to provide local security. This pattern was repeated in a number of other parts of mainland Bougainville during 1991 and 1992. After the PNG government changed leadership in July 1992, the PNG forces took a more aggressive approach, seeking to reestablish control in some areas without first receiving requests from local leaders—the most significant place being the area

7. See Sam Kauona, "Conflict in Bougainville, Part 3: Successes of the Bougainville Revolutionary Army," *NZine*, June 30, 2000, www/nzine.co.nz/features/bville3.html (accessed March 7, 2005); Oliver, *Black Islanders*, 237; and Kemmelfield, "A Short History," 69–70.

around the main urban center of Arawa beginning in late 1992. But even in such areas the PNGDF received support from local armed groups opposed to the BRA. By about 1993 the PNG forces had reasserted a degree of control or influence over perhaps one-third of Bougainville.

During 1992–93 the diverse armed Bougainvillean elements opposing the BRA at the local level began combining as the Bougainville Resistance Forces (BRF), and over time such groups developed closer and semiformal links to the PNG forces and supported the PNGDF in fighting BRA groups. For the most part, the BRA and BRF groups in any particular area were well known to each other—often with close relatives in opposing camps. They were not divided so much by ideology, but more by localized disputes. In the process of conflict over such local issues, however, leaders and many members of the BRF groups tended to become opponents of secession, mainly because they feared that a BRA-controlled government would not look kindly on those who had opposed the BRA. By about 1993 the PNG forces had reasserted a degree of control or influence over perhaps one-third of Bougainville.

Hence, from the early 1990s violent conflict had developed two somewhat distinct dimensions—the secessionist struggle between the BRA and the PNG government, and the internal conflict between opposing Bougainvillean groups. Both dimensions continued until ended by the peace process beginning in July 1997. While these were the most obvious fracture lines, in fact the divisions within and between Bougainville communities were far more complex. Much conflict continued to be at a very localized level, involving old divisions, shifting loyalties, and new disputes over land and other resources. It was not uncommon for former BRA elements that had shown allegiance to the BRF when the PNGDF returned to provide security to an area to later revert to being BRA. There were instances of BRF forces fighting intense conflicts with nearby BRA forces led by close relatives of both forces, while at the same time entering into cooperative arrangements with still other BRA elements in adjoining areas.

Sources of Weapons for the Bougainville Combatant Groups

Because Bougainville is an isolated group of islands, an obvious strategy for the PNG to use in its efforts to defeat the BRA would have been to ensure that no weapons or ammunition reached Bougainville. This was certainly part of the motivation for the blockade of Bougainville imposed by PNG from May 1990. But such a strategy was ineffective in that the BRA never relied on imported weapons and ammunition. In the early stages of the conflict (1988–90), BRA members made extensive use of a few hunting weapons (.22 and .303 rifles) that they were able to locate, as well as knives, bows and arrows, and a range of other improvised weapons. At the same time they concentrated on engaging as much as possible with small police and PNGDF elements, as described by the BRA military commander Sam Kauona: "In the first stage of the fighting, patrols from the PNG forces were ambushed and the Bougainvilleans captured weapons of a high standard—M16s, self loading rifles (SLR), M79 Grenade Launchers, and ammunition. This became the means of the BRA acquiring arms and re-supplying its men. The BRA never imported or bought any arms from abroad."[8]

But the PNG's strategy to prevent weapons reaching armed groups perhaps was chiefly undermined by the availability of two significant sources of weapons within Bougainville. The first involved dumps of World War II weapons, ammunition, and explosives that the BRA was able to retrieve. The second involved homemade weapons designed to use (in the main) the various kinds of caliber of the World War II ammunition. Concerning World War II material, the BRA put a great deal of effort into locating it, particularly after the initial withdrawal of the PNG forces in March 1990. The main dumps were to be found within the area of the former U.S. and Australian base at Torokina, on the west coast of Bougainville, and a former Japanese base at Patupatuai near Buin, in south Bougainville (see Map 4). From 1990 to 1997 some hundreds of weapons were recovered, including heavy machine and submachine guns and rifles, together with tens of thousands of rounds of ammunition. The BRA established workshops, mainly employing former BCL-trained metal workers, who cleaned and repaired such weapons. In addition, the

8. Kauona, "Conflict in Bougainville."

workshops manufactured homemade weapons from steel pipe of various sizes. The ammunition they were designed to use (including 50-caliber rounds) was found in large quantities, especially at Torokina. Large amounts of ammunition located in freshwater (there were lakes, swamps, and rivers in the area of the former base into which much material had been dumped when U.S. forces left in 1944 and Australian forces left at the end of World War II), as opposed to saltwater swamps or earth pits, was found usable. Unexploded bombs were also used to make improvised land mines for use against the PNG forces.

As for the BRF, former BRA elements joining this force usually brought with them whatever weapons that they had amassed while part of the BRA. In addition, the PNGDF and the police riot squads supplied them with modern weapons and ammunition, and they also sometimes captured weapons in clashes with BRA elements (and vice versa).

Some Impacts of the Conflict

Among the terrible outcomes of the conflict for Bougainville was the trauma resulting from perhaps several thousand deaths (probably well over 1,000 Bougainvilleans died in the process of armed conflict, many more from extrajudicial killings on all sides, and an unknown number as a result of the PNG blockade of BRA-controlled areas) and injuries; deep divisions among Bougainvilleans; destruction of most public infrastructure and private sector productive assets; destruction of the capacity of the local state (the Bougainville provincial government's administrative arm); and large-scale dislocation for huge numbers, with up to 60,000 of Bougainville's population, then about 160,000, living in refugee camps by 1996. By the time the peace process began, Bougainville had gone from its preconflict status as the wealthiest of PNG's 19 provinces to among the most impoverished. For PNG, the impacts included perhaps 300 combat deaths and many more injuries, massive economic effects through closure of the mine (which until 1989 had contributed about 17 percent of government revenues and 36 percent of gross export earnings), and serious impacts on the capacity of the state, including serious undermining of the morale of the security forces (in constant crisis from 1989 to 1997). More generally, the conflict resulted in deep divisions and grave distrust between PNG and the elements making up the BRA and its government, as well as between many other groups in Bougainville.

3

The Peace Process, 1997 to 2005—An Overview

The peace process is generally regarded as having begun in mid-1997 (though as discussed shortly, its origins can be traced to initiatives taken at least two years earlier) and can perhaps best be understood as involving three main phases.[1] The first involved establishing the process, June 1997 to June 1999, a phase in which the focus was not on outcomes such as a political settlement, but rather on process. The institutional architecture of the negotiations had to be developed. Deeply distrustful opposing parties needed to feel secure enough to begin developing trust and confidence in the process to a point where they could begin to negotiate a political settlement with their opponents.

The second phase involved negotiating such a settlement. Not surprisingly, this included a long and tortuous process taking over two years, from June 1999 until August 2001, when the Bougainville Peace Agreement was signed.

The third phase involved implementing the political settlement, something beginning virtually as soon as the peace agreement was signed, and in many ways continuing at the time of this writing (early

1. It is not possible here to present a detailed analysis of the various phases, dynamics, and impacts of the peace process. More detailed discussion can be found in Wehner and Denoon, eds., *Without a Gun;* Rebecca Adams, ed., *Peace on Bougainville: Truce Monitoring Group, Gudpela Nius Bilong Pis* (Wellington: Victoria University Press, 2001); Anthony J. Regan, "The Bougainville Political Settlement and the Prospects for Sustainable Peace," *Pacific Economic Bulletin*, vol. 17, no. 1 (2002), 114–29; Andy Carl and Lorraine Garasu, eds., *Weaving Consensus: The Papua New Guinea–Bougainville Peace Process, Accord*, no. 12 (London: Conciliation Resources, 2002); Volker Boege and Lorraine Garasu, "Papua New Guinea: A Success Story of Postconflict Peacebuilding in Bougainville," in Annelies Heijman, Nicola Simmonds, and Hans van de Veen, eds., *Searching for Peace in Asia Pacific: An Overview of Conflict Prevention and Peacebuilding Activities* (Boulder, Colo.: Lynne Rienner, 2004), 564–79; Ron May, "The Bougainville Conflict and Its Resolution," in John Henderson and Greg Watson, eds., *Securing a Peaceful Pacific* (Canterbury: Canterbury University Press, 2005), 459–69; Roger Mortlock, "Lessons from Bougainville," in Henderson and Watson, *Securing a Peaceful Pacific*, 470–74; John Hayes, "Bringing Peace to Bougainville," in Henderson and Watson, *Securing a Peaceful Pacific*, 140–49.

2010). However, for the sake of managing the discussion in this chapter, the peace process will be treated as ending in mid-2005, when the United Nations observer mission left Bougainville. That date is significant here simply because it was when the last part of the monitoring mechanisms in the international intervention ceased operating. Of course, implementation of the peace agreement continued after mid-2005, as discussed in chapter 5.

It is necessary to distinguish between, on the one hand, the formal peace process that began in mid-1997 and, on the other hand, a wide range of local reconciliation efforts in Bougainville intended to resolve localized conflict. The focus of much discussion of the peace process naturally tends to be on the success of the former. But the formal process was to a large degree built on the significant efforts made in relation to the latter, as discussed a little later in this chapter.

More generally, the process had to take account of the complex divisions among Bougainvilleans, not only the general division between pro-secessionist BRA and BIG, on the one hand, and the generally pro-integration BRF, on the other hand, but also the diverse localized divisions already mentioned. As a result, as the peace process developed, it was not a matter of two opposing senior leadership groups agreeing to negotiate on behalf of organized followers. Rather, there was a bewildering proliferation of often localized understandings of and responses to the conflict and the peace process. Further, while most of the BRA and BRF leaders and groups supported the peace process, there were some—mainly associated with original BRA leader Francis Ona—who were initially ambivalent and by early 1998 quite openly opposed to the peace process.

There were similar divisions and uncertainties at the national level. Examples were enumerated in the overview of the conflict in chapter 2: state services on occasion opposed political direction, as occurred when the police withdrew from Bougainville in March 1990 against government wishes; there were public disputes on Bougainville policy within the PNG cabinet, as occurred with the declaration of the blockade over Bougainville in May 1990; and there were significant shifts in policy when governments changed, as occurred in mid-1992. These examples were typical of a complex division of responsibilities in a new postcolonial state where coordination of policy and of state services has always presented difficulties. The situation did not change in later stages of the conflict or in the early stages of the peace process. The scenario in mid-1997 made it difficult for the newly elected political leaders committed to and engaged in the peace process to chart a consistent course.

Origins of the Formal Peace Process

The peace process begun in mid-1997 was really an extension of efforts initiated by moderate Bougainvillean leaders in 1995 to build dialogue between opposing factions through talks facilitated by the Australian government in Cairns (see Map 1) in September and December 1995. These talks had involved representatives of the United Nations and the Commonwealth Secretariat.[2] The talks succeeded in opening intra-Bougainville dialogue, but made little progress toward agreeing how to end the conflict, although it was agreed to meet again in the first part of 1996. But any progress made was disrupted when PNG forces ambushed Bougainvillean leaders returning from Cairns in January 1996, leading to escalating violence for much of that year. However, developments late in 1996 and early 1997 unexpectedly opened the door to a resumption of those talks, as is discussed later in this chapter (see "Main Steps in the Formal Process").

It should be noted that the 1995 talks had built on a number of earlier peace efforts undertaken since 1989—the BRA and other Bougainville leaders as well as the PNG government had all made efforts to engage at various points. Among the earliest had been attempts by Bougainville provincial government leaders and members of the PNG parliament in 1989 to negotiate with Francis Ona, and by the PNG and provincial governments together to propose both a significant redistribution of BCL revenue in favor of Bougainville interests and much increased autonomy for Bougainville.[3] In the end, such initiatives were seen by the BRA leadership as too little and too late.

2. The Commonwealth Secretariat is the coordinating body for the British Commonwealth of Nations, the association of 53 independent states almost all of which were previously part of the British Empire or a territory of a country once part of that Empire. PNG is part of the British Commonwealth and receives some technical and other assistance from the Commonwealth Secretariat.

3. See Oliver, *Black Islanders*, 212–22.

From 1990 the international community had gradually become involved in peace initiatives in Bougainville, in part because Bougainville leaders had begun to establish international links, and in part because particular officials from neighboring countries (as discussed below) and international organizations had shown an interest in interceding. Examples of these efforts include the March 1990 ceasefire that led to the temporary withdrawal of PNG forces already mentioned.[4] Talks between the BRA/BIG leadership and PNG facilitated by the New Zealand government were held on a New Zealand naval ship anchored off Bougainville in mid-1990. New Zealand's ambassador to PNG at the time, John Hayes, played a major role here, in the process gaining insights and relationships that he later made good use of in helping to facilitate the initiation of the peace process in 1997. The Solomon Islands government hosted talks in its capital Honiara in January 1991.[5]

The previous peace initiative that ultimately made the greatest contribution toward the peace process beginning in 1997 was what had been planned as a major intra-Bougainville peace conference held in the former administrative capital, Arawa (see Map 4), in October 1994. It was preceded by a ceasefire agreed between the BRA and PNG, and security for the conference was provided by a regional peacekeeping force—the South Pacific Peace Keeping Force (SPPKF)—funded and organized mainly by Australia but composed mostly of military personnel from Tonga, Fiji, and Vanuatu, with some New Zealand support (see Map 1 for the locations of these countries).[6] Unfortunately, the PNG government failed to include BRA representatives in negotiations about arrangements for the SPPKF (including a "status of forces" agreement),

4. See Kemmelfield, "A Short History"; Oliver, *Black Islanders*, 235–45; and the introductory comments in Peter Wallensteen, "Conflict Prevention," in Henderson and Watson, eds., *Securing a Peaceful Pacific*, 33–42, at 33.

5. See Oliver, *Black Islanders*, 246–26; Matthew Spriggs and Ron May, "Postscript: August 1990," in May and Spriggs, *The Bougainville Crisis*, 112–18; Matthew Spriggs, "Bougainville Update: August 1990 to May 1991," in Spriggs and Denoon, *The Bougainville Crisis: 1991 Update*, 8–27.

6. Bob Breen, *Giving Peace a Chance: Operation Lagoon, Bougainville, 1994: A Case Study of Military Action and Diplomacy* (Canberra: Strategic and Defence Studies Centre, Australian National University, 2001); Reuben R.E. Bowd, *Doves Over the Pacific: In Pursuit of Peace and Stability in Bougainville* (Loftus, NSW: Australian Military History Press, 2007).

leading the BRA to refuse to participate at the last minute, at least in part due to concerns about security for its leadership.[7] Against the orders of the senior BRA and BIG leaders, a few key BRA figures and a senior adviser to the BIG did attend unofficially.

A United Nations officer also attended the Arawa conference and held informal discussions with leaders from all factions, including the BRA figures in attendance. Hiroko Miyamura's assessment of the difficulties that the BRA/BIG would face in getting international community support for its secessionist agenda clearly had sobering impacts on those who heard it. Miyamura's involvement was largely the result of the close interest in Bougainville shown by a senior officer in the United Nations Department of Political Affairs, Francisc Vendrell, who had lived in PNG in the late 1960s and followed the Bougainville situation closely, maintaining links with a range of leaders from various factions. Vendrell later attended the Bougainville talks in Cairns in December 1995, and from late 1997 to early 1998, he played a significant background role in establishing the United Nations observer mission that operated in Bougainville from 1998 to 2005.

Theodore Miriung was the senior BRA/BIG adviser present at the Arawa peace conference. A lawyer who had previously been a senior Bougainville provincial government official as well as an acting judge of the PNG National Court, Miriung had been working with Francis Ona since the early 1990s, and in the days immediately after the conference collapsed he sought to persuade the BRA/BIG leadership to take advantage of the SPPKF presence and participate in talks with Bougainvillean leaders opposing the BRA/BIG. Upon failing to gain their agreement, Miriung emerged as a key figure seeking to unify moderate Bougainville leadership in the search for peace. In discussion with the PNG government, it was agreed to provide a political vehicle for such leadership by reestablishing Bougainville's provincial government, which had previously been suspended by the PNG government (in 1990). Renamed the Bougainville Transitional Government (BTG)—a name intended to emphasize its intended role in seeking a transition to a new status for Bougainville—it began operating in April 1995, based in Buka Town (see Map 4). Headed by Miriung as premier,

7. Breen, *Giving Peace a Chance*, 58–60.

the BTG sought to bridge the gap between, on the one hand, the BRA/BIG with its commitment to achieving secession through military means and, on the other hand, the BRF and associated leaders increasingly strident in their commitment to supporting the PNGDF to ensure that Bougainville remain reintegrated within the PNG. As a party between these two factions, the BTG (under a new premier, Gerard Sinato) played vital roles in organizing the intra-Bougainville leadership talks held in Cairns in 1995 that were to continue between the opposing Bougainville factions in New Zealand in mid-1997. Despite Miriung's assassination in September 1996 by PNGDF and BRF personnel, the BTG was also a major party in initiating those 1997 talks.

It should be noted that at the time that they occurred, these various peace initiatives—including the 1994 peace conference—were regarded as failures, in that they did not end the conflict. In fact, however, they served as a foundation for the ultimately successful peace process. Among other things, they encouraged the emergence of the moderate Bougainvillean leadership involved in the BTG. Further, the various peace initiatives before 1997 provided vital experience to Bougainville and PNG negotiators and key Australian, New Zealand, and United Nations figures; built understanding of the complex nature of the conflict among the most interested parties of the international community; provided links between international community actors and major figures in the PNG government and the Bougainville factions; permitted exploration of options by leaders on all sides; and excluded approaches that did not work.

Various broader developments in late 1996 and early 1997 also contributed to the initiation of the mid-1997 dialogue. In fact, events had conspired to strengthen the positions of moderate leaders on all sides. Significant among these were the early 1997 efforts of elements of the PNGDF, including the then commander, in getting foreign mercenaries engaged by the PNG government through a British-based company with South African connections, Sandline International. The aim of the PNG government in engaging the mercenaries was to assist the

PNGDF in defeating the BRA and reopening the Panguna mine.[8] The US$36 million contract negotiated in late 1996 and signed in January 1997 involved Sandline supplying high-tech equipment and mercenaries (mainly from Africa) to train and support the PNGDF, in special and what were initially intended to be highly secret operations, to defeat the BRA/BIG (by killing the senior leadership) and take control of the Panguna mine. The mercenaries and a wide range of equipment intended for use in the operation began arriving in Port Moresby early in February 1997, and the mercenaries began training the PNGDF special forces unit almost immediately. Very quickly information about the arrival of Sandline personnel and equipment circulated in PNG and gave rise to grave concern in Australia and other regional capitals about the risks for regional security inherent in governments relying on mercenaries to deal with internal conflict problems. The PNG government faced an escalating crisis both domestically and regionally before the PNGDF commander in mid-March 1997 stepped in to detain the Sandline personnel (subsequently deported) and demand the resignation of the prime minister (Sir Julius Chan) and other key ministers involved in approving the Sandline contract. The motives of the commander for taking this action have never been clear, particularly as he had been fully involved in the PNG government decisionmaking on engaging Sandline in the first place. Nevertheless, the outcomes of his actions were dramatic, resulting in ten days of intense political instability with elements of the military joining popular demonstrations demanding resignation of the government. In late March 1997 the government announced a commission of inquiry into the Sandline affair, and the standing down of the prime minister and the two main ministers involved in the contract, pending the outcome of that inquiry.

Among other things, these developments changed BRA perceptions (particularly of the PNGDF) as to who were its "enemies" and opened opportunities for moderate PNG political leadership interested in

8. On the Sandline mercenary affair and its impacts on the Bougainville conflict and peace process, see Sinclair Dinnen, Ron May, and Anthony J. Regan, eds., *Challenging the State: The Sandline Affair in Papua New Guinea* (Canberra: Asia Pacific Press, 1997); Sean Dorney, *The Sandline Affair: Politics and Mercenaries and the Bougainville Crisis* (Sydney: ABC Books, 1998); Mary Louise O'Callaghan, *Enemies Within: Papua New Guinea, Australia, and the Sandline Crisis: The Inside Story* (Sydney: Doubleday, 1998).

negotiating a political settlement.[9] There was an additional major factor that influenced the BRA/BIG leadership to consider negotiation, namely war weariness, evidence of which had been growing for some time. From at least the mid-1990s concern among moderate leaders had grown about the negative impact of the internal conflict (BRA and BRF) on common Bougainvillean identity and unity that had been developing among the diverse language and culture groups before the conflict. The fear was that a secession achieved by some years more of divisive conflict would ultimately be unsustainable. Such concerns had also been a factor in the emergence of the BTG in 1995 and continued to influence its leadership thereafter. More generally, the long-running conflict and the constant insecurity and danger were causing significant levels of hardship for people in all areas of Bougainville, especially those in BRA/BIG-controlled areas with little access to health and education services. In late 1996 and early 1997, villagers in BRA-controlled areas disobeyed orders from the BIG/BRA leaders against accepting Australian government funded Red Cross humanitarian assistance in the form of "village packs" and "family packs" intended to meet basic needs of people deprived of such things as agricultural tools, seeds, and cooking utensils. For moderate BRA and BIG leaders this development underlined the war weariness of their people, the irrationality of the hard-line leadership associated with Francis Ona, and the risk of long-term divisions that could undermine the viability of secession.

On the PNG side, the failure of the major military operation in 1996 together with strong opposition in the military to the use of the Sandline mercenaries meant that options for military success were largely exhausted. Sandline had other impacts on the PNG government, in that the eruption of what almost amounted to open revolt by a significant part of the PNGDF against the government of the day was a severe shock, underlining the view that the ongoing conflict in Bougainville was inflicting crippling damage on PNG. Prime Minister Chan was replaced by a moderate acting prime minister who supported formal adoption of

9. For a discussion of the impacts of the Sandline mercenary affair on the origins of the Bougainville peace process, see Anthony Regan, "Preparation for War and Progress towards Peace—Bougainville Dimensions of the Sandline Affair," in Dinnen, May, Regan, eds., *Challenging the State*, 82–93.

a peace strategy, including support for renewal of the consultation among Bougainvillean factions blocked by the escalating violence in 1996. The temporary change in PNG leadership (for Chan resumed office as prime minister in June 1997, weeks before general elections in July in which he lost his seat in the PNG parliament) much reduced any likelihood of action by PNG forces to undermine the steps necessary to organize the first negotiations. The July 1997 general elections in fact consolidated the change in PNG's policy on Bougainville, by returning a new prime minister, Bill Skate, who had long been committed to a peaceful resolution of the conflict. He immediately appointed a newly elected Bougainvillean member of parliament, Sam Akoitai, as minister for Bougainville affairs. Like many Bougainvilleans, when the conflict began, Akoitai had been a BRA sympathizer, but when he came under suspicion from local BRA elements, he was forced to protect himself and joined armed opposition to the BRA, eventually becoming chairman of the BRF. In that capacity he became a nominated member of the BTG and close to its peace-seeking premier, Theodore Miriung. In his new role as minister in the PNG government, he pursued Miriung's goal of bringing the divided Bougainville factions together and was able to be especially persuasive in the PNG cabinet in that he had been a fighter with the BRF on the side of the PNG forces. These changes in leadership in the PNG government were among the most significant factors enabling the government to take advantage of the opportunities for peacebuilding in 1997. While for other reasons Skate is not regarded as having been a particularly good prime minister for PNG, he certainly remained committed and made significant contributions to the Bougainville peace process throughout his two years in office.

In summary, by 1997 while the BRA/BIG appeared to have achieved military ascendancy, there was, in fact, a kind of "mutually hurting stalemate" situation for all parties.[10]

10. I. William Zartman, "Ripeness: The Hurting Stalemate and Beyond," in Paul C. Stern and Daniel Druckman, eds. *International Conflict Resolution after the Cold War* (Washington: National Academies Press, 2000); Eric Brahm, "Hurting Stalemate Stage," in Guy Burgess and Heidi Burgess, eds., *Beyond Intractability* (Boulder, Colo.: Conflict Research Consortium, University of Colorado, September 2003) www.beyondintractability.org/essay/stalemate/ (accessed June 1, 2007).

The "Informal" Peace Process—Local Reconciliation and Peacebuilding

In many ways the foundation of the peace process was not so much in the well-publicized steps toward formal meetings of senior leaders of opposing parties and factions as in the myriad local reconciliation and peacebuilding efforts that had been developing in most parts of Bougainville almost as soon as the conflict began and had gathered strength throughout the 1990s.

The resilience of Bougainville's precolonial social structures and norms has already been mentioned, in particular the role of reciprocal exchange in maintaining social order. It must also be stated the the strong pressure to maintain balanced reciprocity creates considerable pressure to restore balance even where it has been disturbed by conflict and violence.

Parties do not automatically agree to work toward restoration of balance. It is necessary first to develop consensus within each group affected by the conflict. Only then can strong social pressure be brought to bear to end the conflict. This usually involves working toward restoration of relationships damaged by conflict, and doing so through mediation culminating in public reconciliation ceremonies where both sides express their concerns and make apologies for wrongs committed in the course of violence. If it is accepted that only one side has been in the wrong, the victim's spokesperson will normally talk about accepting the apology. Compensation is usually offered or gifts exchanged—usually in the form of ceremonial shell money or pigs—although there can also be demands for and/or payment of cash.[11] Ancient symbolic ceremonies mark the end of the conflict, which vary considerably from place to place. They often involve leaders of the reconciling groups breaking and chewing betel nut together and then spitting the betel nut juice into a freshly dug hole (to symbolize the ousting together of the conflict), then placing a stone on top of that (to symbolize the burying of the

11. See Pat Howley, *Breaking Spears and Mending Hearts: Peacemakers & Restorative Justice in Bougainville* (London/Sydney: Zed Books/The Federation Press, 2002), 125–29; Pat Howley, "Restorative Justice in Bougainville," in Sinclair Dinnen with Anita Jowitt and Tess Newton Cain, eds., *A Kind of Mending: Restorative Justice in the Pacific Islands* (Canberra: Pandanus Books, 2003), 237–45.

conflict), and then planting a coconut or fruit tree in the soil used to fill the hole (to symbolize the growth of a new relationship and the fruits that it will deliver). If the conflict has been violent, especially involving the use of weapons, there will also often be a ceremonial breaking of wooden spears or bows and arrows (the weapons of precolonial Bougainville). Such practices increasingly also reflect the strong influence of Christianity in Bougainville (for example, through prayers, prominent roles for priests and pastors, use of rosary beads where the Catholic religion is strong, or provision of bibles or prayer books, any of which may be prominent as apologies are made and accepted). These—in many ways "hybrid"—practices are nevertheless regarded as essentially based in Bougainville custom and, as a result, have far more efficacy in resolution of conflict and wrongs committed during conflict than the formal courts established by the state. Even in the years preceding the conflict, the majority of conflicts within and between Bougainvillean communities involving what would readily be classified as criminal offenses under PNG law were regarded by most communities more as incidents damaging relationships and balanced reciprocity, and therefore better dealt with through these hybrid reconciliation processes directed at restoring relationships and balanced reciprocity rather than through the state legal system.

Consensus can be difficult to achieve, however, especially among social groups without strong, hierarchical leadership. First, to end a conflict all parties must usually have an incentive to reconcile before they will negotiate, such as all feeling threatened in some way by the ongoing violence. If one group feels that it has grounds to feel particularly aggrieved or that it has a strong advantage over the others, it may have little incentive to explore mediation and reconciliation as a means of ending the conflict. Situations are further complicated where longstanding enmities exist between groups. If conflict flares again, it can be very difficult to find a mediated settlement. More generally, mediation and reconciliation involving customary practices are more readily entertained as a means of dealing with conflicts between groups that have a history of interaction and share similar customs (for example, neighboring groups or groups with trading or other relationships). In the period since colonial rule, Bougainvillean groups have increasingly interacted with others with whom they had previously not related, and where conflict occurs between such groups it is not always easy to use customary mediation processes. Of course, during and after the years of conflict being discussed here, interactions between individuals and groups have perhaps been more complex and intense than at any time in Bougainville's history. Often language groups have been separated by considerable distances and seldom came into contact before the conflict, circumstances that made customary or "hybrid" reconciliation processes more difficult.

When cases include extreme violence, anger and hurt (over injuries, deaths, and loss of property), consensus can be even harder to attain. Parties can simply refuse to participate. Further, the efficacy of conflict resolution using customary mediation and reconciliation can vary a great deal between areas. For example, local conflict in south Bougainville in the period from 1992 to 1997 was probably more intense than in central and north Bougainville, perhaps due to local land and other pressure, and perhaps even to cultural differences between the south and other areas. Whatever the reasons, the intensity of conflict, combined with factors already cited, seems to have made ending local conflict in the south using mediation and reconciliation even more complex than elsewhere. And those difficulties, which in turn contributed to there being many more unreconciled conflicts in south Bougainville than elsewhere by the time the UN mission left in mid-2005, have been a significant factor in localized conflict resuming in that area after 2005, as outlined in chapter 6.

Despite these significant caveats about the efficacy of customary and hybrid reconciliation efforts, it is also true that during the 1990s many local leaders played important roles in many (though not all) parts of Bougainville in resolving conflict between individuals and groups.[12] The leaders included traditional "chiefs" (mainly males), church leaders,

12. For a discussion of reconciliation efforts in Bougainville, see Howley, *Breaking Spears*, and "Restorative Justice"; John Tombot, "A Marriage of Custom and Introduced Skills: Restorative Justice Bougainville Style," in Dinnen, Jowitt, and Cain, eds., *A Kind of Mending*, 255–64; and for a description by a BIG/BRA leader of reconciliation processes and efforts undertaken under the auspices of the BIG/BRA leadership from late 1996, see James Tanis, "Reconciliation: My Side of the Island," in Carl and Garasu, eds., *Weaving Consensus*, 58–61.

and others. Women's leaders and groups also initiated many such efforts, sometimes drawing on long-established, traditional dispute-settlement roles of women, which many Bougainvilleans assert are particularly strong in predominantly matrilineal Bougainville (though that is not to say that Bougainvillean women are any more inherently peaceful than women elsewhere).[13]

A strong interest in returning to traditional ways of doing things well served the conflict resolution efforts under consideration here. The absence of state authority in much of Bougainville for long periods between 1990 and 1997 (and beyond in some parts) meant people in many areas looked to traditional chiefs and clan leaders to fill the vacuum in local decisionmaking structures. The tendency to increasingly utilize modified traditional approaches to resolving conflict was thus part of a wider tendency to rely more heavily on precolonial social structures and contributed to those approaches becoming a fundamentally important part of local reconciliation and peacebuilding efforts. The fact that such efforts were regarded as largely "traditional" gave them enhanced legitimacy in the eyes of all Bougainvilleans, most of whom agreed on the importance of restoring traditions that had weakened since colonial rule. Community members supporting peace drew strength and legitimacy through widespread community support for such efforts, which in many ways laid the foundation for the broader peace process.

Community-level activities provided a basis for involvement of a major Port Moresby–based non-governmental organization (NGO) (Peace Melanesia) undertaking a great deal of mediation and reconciliation training work intended to support local initiatives,[14] and the

13. Lorraine Garasu, "Women Promoting Peace and Reconciliation," in Carl and Garasu, eds., *Weaving Consensus*, 28–31; Ruth Saovana-Spriggs, "Bougainville Women's Role in Conflict Resolution in the Bougainville Peace Process," in Dinnen, Jowitt, and Cain, eds., *A Kind of Mending*, 195–214; Marylin Taleo Havini and Josephine Takunani Sirivi, eds., *As Mothers of the Land: The Birth of Bougainville Women for Peace and Freedom* (Canberra: Pandanus Books, 2004); UNIFEM, "Case Study: Bougainville—Papua New Guinea," www.womenwarpeace.org/webfm_send/191 (accessed August 27, 2008); Ruth Saovana-Spriggs, "Gender and Peace: Bougainvillean Women, Matriliny, and the Peace Process," Ph.d. dissertation (Australian National University, Canberra, 2007). See also Hilary Charlesworth, "Are Women Peaceful: Reflections on the Role of Women in Peace Building," *Feminist Legal Studies*, vol. 16 (2008): 347–61.

14. Ibid.

development of a range of homegrown Bougainvillean organizations (locally initiated NGOs mainly funded by foreign donors) that encouraged conflict resolution and/or sought an end to the violence. Several such bodies were established and led by educated women, who in part drew upon perceptions of the importance of women's customary peacemaking roles to provide legitimacy for their efforts to assert themselves in the public arena commonly regarded as a male preserve. Far from being a matter of traditional custom, they were in fact largely engaged in the thoroughly "modern" struggle to assert the human rights of women to share in the exercise of public authority. They were challenging the patriarchal side of Bougainville social structures (and continue to do so at the time of this writing).

During the latter years of the conflict, together the factors just discussed not only pressured those leaders committed to military solutions to consider alternatives, but also enabled an emerging moderate leadership among the opposing factions. They also helped to strengthen Bougainvillean civil society, a matter discussed later in this monograph. That societies in the rest of PNG tend to share similar cultural practices to those found in Bougainville meant that at the PNG national level, many leaders (both political and bureaucratic) were similarly open to the possibility of reconciliation and, to some extent, understood the peace process in those terms.

From the very beginning of the peace process in mid-1997, the importance of the local roles played by Bougainville chiefs and leaders of women's and other community organizations was recognized through their inclusion in major negotiating sessions held in New Zealand and Australia, and in various ways this continued throughout the first two years.[15] This established linkages between, on the one hand, localized processes well understood by the communities, and, on the other hand, the more formal and far more remote "official" peace process. These linkages greatly enhanced not only the understanding of ordinary Bougainvilleans of the wider process, but also the legitimacy of the Bougainville Peace Agreement signed between PNG and the Bougainville parties in August 2001.

15. Ibid.

There was a significant exception, however, to the continuity of inclusivity of leadership in the various phases of the peace process. For two years, from June 1999 to August 2001, leaders of women's groups had almost no involvement in the large Bougainville team that negotiated the final peace agreement, there being at least two main reasons. First, the political negotiations were seen as largely involving the main Bougainville factions, whose leadership was almost exclusively male, thereby reflecting the patriarchal aspect of Bougainville social structures. Second, much of that leadership viewed the traditional peacemaking role of women as being over once the violence had ended and wanted the women to return to customary roles, leaving male leaders to occupy the public political space. Patriarchy was asserted over matriliny, a rebuff for the educated women seeking to increase public leadership roles for women.

Main Steps in the Formal Process

The optimism for exploring peace, after the Sandline mercenaries had been ejected in early in 1997 (see earlier discussion), quickly gave way to the reality that a secure peace process would be difficult to achieve. From the beginning, however, peace rested in the hands of key actors—leaders of Bougainvillean factions and the PNG government—with encouragement and facilitation from particular international community actors. In the initial phases this especially involved New Zealand government officials, involved in peace initiatives from late in 1996.

A flurry of activity in April, May, and June 1997, facilitated and mediated by the New Zealand government with active Australian support, led to the resumption of talks (begun in Cairns in December 1995) among the opposing Bougainville factions (at this stage the focus was on intra-Bougainville talks, it being regarded as too early for the divided Bougainvilleans to begin engaging with PNG). The talks took place at military barracks in Burnham, New Zealand (see Map 1), after Solomon Islands was rejected as a venue because of security concerns.[16] The talks

16. Nigel Moore, "New Zealand in the Bougainville Peace Process," notes of a seminar presentation to the State, Society, and Governance in Melanesia Program seminar series, Australian National University, May 8, 2001, http://rspas.anu.edu.au/papers/melanesia/seminars/nigelmoore8may01.php (accessed June 26, 2009).

involved representatives of the BRA, BIG, BTG, and BRF, together with representatives of the churches in Bougainville and of the local NGOs (including women's organizations). In addition, a few prominent Bougainvilleans asked to attend in their own right. The total number of Bougainvillean "delegates" was almost 100. From the outset, John Hayes, the former New Zealand ambassador to PNG, who in 1997 was a senior official responsible for Pacific Island Affairs in the New Zealand Ministry of Foreign Affairs and Trade, helped to organize the talks. In doing so he spent a considerable amount of time in Bougainville encouraging a wide range of leaders to attend. The New Zealand government arranged their travel and attendance. Together with New Zealand's minister for foreign affairs, Don Mackinnon, Hayes played significant encouragement and (on occasion) mediation roles at the talks.[17] Two weeks of talks resulted in the Burnham Declaration of July 18, 1997, in which the main Bougainville factions agreed to work together toward peace with PNG.[18]

Despite agreeing to work together, the positions of the main Bougainville parties attending the Burnham talks continued to be deeply divided. The BIG and BRA sought recognition of the UDI, as declared by Francis Ona in May 1990, or at the very least the earliest possible internationally supervised and binding referendum for Bougainvilleans on independence of Bougainville from PNG. The BTG and BRF opposed independence, for the most part because of fear that independence under a BRA-dominated government would result in an anarchic situation similar to that which had occurred when PNG forces left Bougainville after the March 1990 ceasefire. So while agreement by those parties to work together was seen as a positive step, it was far from clear then that a unifying political agenda could ever be agreed between the opposing Bougainville factions.

After Bill Skate became PNG prime minister in July 1997, some time was taken for the new government to consolidate a growing consensus

17. For more discussion of the New Zealand government role in the early stages of the process, see Roger Mortlock, "A Good Thing to Do," in Adams, ed., *Peace on Bougainville*, 69–82; Joseph Kabui, "Reconciliation A Priori," in Adams, ed., *Peace on Bougainville*, 33–44; John Hayes, "Bringing Peace to Bougainville."

18. Ibid.

for peace, which opened the way to talks between officials for the PNG government and the Bougainville factions that began in October 1997, again at Burnham Barracks in New Zealand. A truce—the Burnham Truce—was agreed to, which included establishing a neutral monitoring force.[19] Very soon after, a joint New Zealand and Australian resource group (comprising military and civilian personnel) spent 10 days in Port Moresby and Bougainville scoping the tasks and requirements for the proposed monitoring force. There followed extensive consultations between New Zealand and Australian officials with the PNG government, as well as with governments of two other countries contributing to the monitoring force (Fiji and Vanuatu) and Bougainville leaders. The initial architecture for mechanisms and processes to both manage and support the peace process emerged during talks between Bougainville and PNG officials and advisers in Cairns, Australia, in late November. It was here that the parties agreed to establish an unarmed regional truce and ceasefire monitoring group—the Truce Monitoring Group (TMG)—intended to provide the secure atmosphere in which they could gradually build trust in one another and confidence in the process (the TMG's role and performance are discussed in chapter 4).[20] In early December the four countries contributing to the TMG signed a multilateral agreement with PNG on the group's mandate and formal arrangements.[21] The basic components needed for the peace process as outlined through these meetings included

- mechanisms established by the PNG and Bougainville parties in order to manage both their developing relationships and the process more generally,
- an international intervention comprising several distinct components, and

19. Ibid.

20. The full text of the Cairns Commitment of November 24, 1997, is available at www.c-r.org/our-work/accord/png-bougainville/key-texts17.php (accessed August 10, 2009).

21. The full text of the agreement, dated December 5, 1997, among New Zealand, PNG, Australia, Fiji, and Vanuatu that provided the framework for the operation of the TMG, is reproduced in Wehner and Denoon, *Without a Gun*, appendix D, at 165–84.

- mechanisms and processes by which the local actors managed the international intervention and integrated it into the peace process.

All of the above are discussed in more detail later in this monograph. These mechanisms and processes, of course, developed and changed as the peace process itself developed.

By the end of 1997 there had been no meeting between PNG and Bougainville political leaders, but rather meetings among combatants, officials, and advisers. The focus of agreements in October and November was on technical details needed to support the truce. In January 1998 the political leaders of the main opposing parties (PNG, BRA/BIG, BTG, and BRF), as well as Bougainville community leaders, met at Lincoln University in New Zealand (see Map 1) to discuss a broad road map for the next steps in the process. Set out in the Lincoln Agreement of January 1998, the steps were in general implemented as agreed, although the ambitious timetable in the agreement was not always adhered to.[22] Major steps taken with the dates accomplished include: negotiating an "irrevocable" ceasefire (February 1998 through signing at the end of April 1998); monitoring the ceasefire through use of a continuing regional group until the ceasefire's full operation at the beginning of May 1998, when the TMG would become the Peace Monitoring Group (PMG); establishing a UN observer mission (August 1998); developing a unifying "Bougainville reconciliation government" (mid-1998 to mid-1999), the expectation being that such a government would assist the divided Bougainvilleans to work together and develop a united negotiating position; and negotiating a political agreement between the Bougainville factions and PNG (June 1999 to August 2001).

The last two steps took far longer than anticipated, to a large extent because of increasing tensions among the still fragile coalition of previously opposed Bougainvillean factions that were supporting the peace process. These tensions resulted largely from competition for power arising from the opportunities created by moves toward establishing the "reconciliation government," so called in the Lincoln Agreement (matters discussed below under "Fragility of the Process and Divisions

22. Ibid.

among Bougainvilleans"). As a result, significant elements of the Bougainvillean factions favoring continued integration into PNG refused to participate in the development of the mainly elected reconciliation government. Despite their objections, such a government was established in May 1999 and called the Bougainville People's Congress (BPC). The pro-integration leaders also refused to participate in the first round of negotiations for a political settlement held between PNG and the BPC on June 30, 1999, although compromises made later that year saw them join all subsequent rounds of negotiations. Despite these temporary difficulties, the installation of the BPC was a significant step forward; despite the absence of dissident pro-integration leaders, it did bring together many leaders of the opposing political factions and armed groups into a single political entity.

Under the Lincoln Agreement road map, the reconciliation government was necessary before political negotiations could begin, and so from this point the focus of the peace process moved from one of efforts to establish the process to one of achieving outcomes on the major political issues dividing the parties. These negotiations continued for more than two years until August 30, 2001, when a comprehensive political settlement with PNG was signed—the Bougainville Peace Agreement. At that point the focus of the process moved to implementation of the agreement, something better discussed after the main features of the peace agreement have been outlined (see chapter 5).

Fragility of the Process and Divisions among Bougainvilleans

As might be expected, the deep mistrust on all sides made the peace process extremely fragile in its early stages. In addition, however, divisions and tensions among the senior leadership of the Bougainville factions, evident during the conflict, continued and became more complex. In combination with more localized divisions and conflict, such factors created major challenges for those managing and supporting the process. Aspects of leadership divisions during the conflict have already been touched on but require brief elaboration, both because they underline the difficulties involved in developing and managing the peace process and because they point to underlying sources of conflict that have had continued significance in later phases of the process (see chapter 6). More generally, this discussion underlines the point often made in relation to conflicts—that they seldom, if ever, end entirely when a peace process is finalized, even those regarded as successful. Rather, conflict normally continues in some form or another, even after a successful negotiation reduces violence. As discussed later, some violent armed conflict that is in many ways linked to the 1988–97 conflict has been ongoing in Bougainville, continuing even to the time of this writing.

Sources and Signs of Fragility

The fragility and uncertainty of the situation, which was particularly difficult for the first 18 months or so after July 1997, were contributing factors to the divisions and tensions in Bougainville. Because of past unsuccessful or only partially successful peace efforts, there was little sense of certainty or inevitability about this process succeeding. Indeed, a senior Australian official working with the TMG early in 1998 has observed that initially "all groups expected the Truce to collapse, like previous ceasefires. Francis Ona was convinced that the peace process would fail without him. The BIG/BRA, PNGDF and Resistance also expected it to fall over—the only question was what would trigger its collapse."[23] Tensions and mistrust between the opposing armed groups remained high. The PNG security forces were both deeply suspicious of the BRA and not fully under control of the PNG political leadership, factors that help to explain why an ambush was planned by PNG forces on BRA/BIG leaders returning from the Burnham talks in New Zealand in July 1997 (it was avoided because of good New Zealand intelligence). Further a moderate delegate with BRA links was murdered soon after his return from New Zealand, with PNG forces widely suspected of involvement. These and other lesser incidents occurred before the TMG was established (late November 1997), at which point the security situation improved dramatically, for even though the TMG was unarmed, its presence provided significant reassurance to all parties concerning risks of insecurity. Even so, there were constant rumors and allegations that one armed group or another was preparing for action

23. Rhys Puddicombe, "Role of the Chief Negotiator," in Wehner and Denoon, *Without a Gun*, 62–69, at 63.

against another. Although the TMG and the PMG played important roles in resolving the resulting difficulties, and generally helped increase the trust between the armed groups, it was a slow process.[24]

Divisions on the "Left"—The Pro-Secession Dissidents

From the earliest stages of the peace process, there were differences among the senior BIG/BRA leaders about their negotiating position and strategy. Although they agreed on the ultimate goal of independence, their original leader, Francis Ona, and his closest advisers maintained that Bougainville was in fact already independent under the terms of the UDI of May 1990. On the other hand, Ona's deputy (vice president of the BIG and former premier of the North Solomons Provincial Government), Joseph Kabui, together with most senior BRA leaders who attended the New Zealand talks, instead pursued international recognition of the UDI or agreement to a process directed to achieving independence in the near future. In terms of strategy, from the outset Ona was at best ambivalent about the wisdom of engaging in the July 1997 New Zealand talks. He faced conflicting advice in that regard. While Kabui and others were positive in their assessment of the possibilities of engaging first with opposing Bougainvillean factions and then PNG, other key advisers argued that the problems of the PNG government in early to mid-1997 arising from the Sandline mercenary crisis should not be seen so much as an opportunity to resume discussions with PNG at that time, but rather offered the possibility that PNG would eventually emerge utterly exhausted and so at a much later point could be expected to be ready to negotiate a deal very much to Ona's advantage.[25] Initially Ona tentatively agreed to Joseph Kabui's proposal to go to Solomon Islands, and then New Zealand for the Burnham talks,[26] but while Kabui and other BRA and BIG leaders were in New Zealand, the opponents of the talks who remained with Ona took the opportunity to persuade him that it was not then time to negotiate and that Kabui was undermining the BIG/BRA's chances of ultimate

24. Ibid.

25. Reuben Siara, "The Time Is Now," in Adams, ed., *Peace on Bougainville*, 125–30, at 126.

26. Kabui, "Reconciliation," 36–7; Siara, "The Time Is Now."

success. By the time Kabui returned, Ona's attitude had firmed into one of strong opposition to the process. In part, his attitude may have been the result of his feeling threatened that through engaging in the New Zealand talks, Kabui might gain enhanced leadership status, sufficient to challenge Ona's authority. But Ona also held an unrealistic view of his own importance as the key Bougainvillean leader. He never understood the extent to which his credibility was eroded by his hard-line stand on independence, at a time when war weariness and other factors already discussed were contributing to a strong and growing Bougainvillean constituency for a negotiated settlement.[27] In fact, with the vast majority of the BRA leadership and its armed units, as well as the chiefs and many clan leaders in most communities supporting Kabui and the peace initiatives, Kabui was in a strong position.

Ona did retain strong community support in his home area around the Panguna mine and in a minority of communities in various parts of Bougainville (the main areas where he retained support are shown as "Me'ekamui/MDF support areas" in Map 6). He also retained some support among a minority of the elements of the armed BRA companies in various parts of Bougainville—generally the parts of BRA units based in the communities that continued to support him. Although he was aware that he did not have the firepower to challenge Kabui and the majority of the BIG/BRA leaders supporting the peace process, Ona could nevertheless have expected that the fragility of the process was such that support would readily swing back to him. Hoping to win over wavering citizens in the lead-up to the signing of the ceasefire in April 1998, for instance, he announced that in view of the UDI he had declared in May 1990, Bougainville was already independent and was to henceforth be called the Republic of Me'ekamui—"sacred land" in his Nasioi language—and that the former BRA elements still loyal to him were now designated the Me'ekamui Defense Force (MDF). Conscious of the consolidation of public support behind more moderate leadership and, in particular, knowing that there was strong BRA support for the peace process, Ona must have been aware that his options were limited. In a confrontation with the BRA, he could not have expected the scattered, armed MDF elements to prevail, and there is no evidence that he

27. Interviews with Joseph Kabui (September 2003) and James Tanis (August 2001).

ever considered such a course. He had little choice but to indicate that while he opposed the peace process, he would not take action against it, retaining hope that in time he could win more support.

The communities whose leaders supported Ona constituted perhaps 10 to 15 percent of the population, with their main concentration in a mountainous area of about 8,000 people in a number of villages near the closed mine at Panguna. The area was originally designated by the TMG and the PMG as a "no-go-zone" for their helicopters and motor vehicles carrying monitoring teams—a force protection measure. Ona subsequently adopted the "no-go-zone" as his own, restricting access by a roadblock operated by other armed MDF personnel stationed at the Morgan Junction (where the only road into the area joins the trunk road along the populous east coast of Bougainville, see Map 6). On several occasions he announced significant expansions of the "zone," but these had little practical impact other than to encourage some other armed MDF roadblocks on the main coastal trunk road, which were at times a considerable irritant to the PMG and the Bougainville provincial government, particularly one set up for several periods at Aropa on the trunk road between Arawa and Buin. Basic government health and education services were not permitted in the "no-go-zone". The former BRA "A" company was based in the "no-go-zone" and became part of the MDF, while in other areas, former BRA elements based in communities that supported Ona often also became part of the MDF.

Although community support for Ona's continued opposition to the peace process never increased significantly, he continued to have high stature among a majority of Bougainvilleans until his death in July 2005, and his often-strident public opposition to the peace process put pressure on BRA and BIG leaders supporting it. He was a constant warning that they could rapidly lose support if the process did not produce results acceptable to the majority of people. At the same time, those same leaders were able to utilize his opposition to the process as part of their negotiating strategy, especially during the protracted negotiations with the PNG government concerning a political settlement, for they were always able to warn opponents during negotiations (both pro-PNG Bougainvillean elements and PNG government representatives) of the dangers of support flowing back to Ona if Kabui and his supporters did not maintain their position concerning rapid progress to independence.

Divisions on the "Right"—The Pro-Integration Dissidents

The divisions among the Bougainville leaders occurred on both sides of the ideological divide, not just among the pro-independence groups that might be regarded as constituting the "left" of Bougainville politics. As already discussed, late in 1998 and 1999 divisions emerged among those one might call the "right" (those favoring maintaining integration into PNG) over the structure and method of establishing the reconciliation government proposed under the Lincoln Agreement. The prospect that long-term political advantage might be gained through control of even such an interim government precipitated intense competition among the Bougainvillean groups supporting the peace process. A complex 18-month power struggle developed from mid-1998, largely because leaders of some groups supporting Bougainville's integration into PNG became concerned that the BRA/BIG elements might gain political advantage through elections for the interim reconciliation government. These leaders included a major part of the senior leadership of the BRF, the influential local government for Buka Island (the Leitana Council of Elders), and three of Bougainville's four members in the National Parliament (the fourth, Sam Akoitai, was the minister responsible for Bougainville matters in the PNG government and supported the proposals for a mainly elected Bougainville reconciliation government).

When legislative steps toward establishing an elected reconciliation government were unexpectedly blocked in December 1998, the dissident group, under a senior Bougainville member of parliament, John Momis, proposed an alternative. The 1995 reforms to the PNG-wide provincial government system that had yet to be applied to Bougainville should come into force on January 1, 1999, and Momis should become governor, heading a new provincial government, consisting of nominated members that would replace the BTG. This proposal was completely unexpected, and at the time it was made, it was not understood by either the PNG government or the more moderate Bougainville leaders that it was being supported by a significant leadership group. Rather, the immediate focus was on the reaction of the BRA and BIG leadership to the legislative blocking of the arrangements for establishing the mainly elected reconciliation government that they had been supporting. The BRA and BIG leaders were deeply concerned at this development. Some feared it would place Momis in real control of Bougainville, very much to the advantage of the pro-integration elements of the Bougainville leadership. More important, this move was seen as a rejection of the progress already made toward agreement on establishing a broadly inclusive reconciliation government under the Lincoln Agreement. Angry BIG/BRA leaders threatened to walk away from the process. A compromise, hastily negotiated between advisers to PNG and the moderate leadership, involved the PNG government

- suspending the arrangements for the new provincial government system in Bougainville;
- agreeing to recognize a reconciliation government (the BPC) established mainly through elections and in part by nominations from significant factions and interests, though without a formal legal basis; and
- agreeing to exercise the powers of the suspended provincial government solely on advice of the BPC.

Dismayed that Momis was not to automatically become governor, the dissident pro-integration leaders refused to work with the broad coalition that worked to establish the BPC, which began operating in May 1999 with Ona's former deputy, Joseph Kabui, elected as president.

This confrontation from late 1998, which was not resolved until late 1999, seemed to potentially threaten the peace process. But, in fact, it gradually became clear that a large part of the more moderate pro-integration leadership was supporting the BPC and moving closer to the moderate BRA/BIG leadership associated with Kabui, leaving the dissident pro-integration leaders feeling increasingly isolated. On the other hand, the broader coalition of moderate leadership in the BPC could not ignore the pro-integration dissidents. Apart from anything else, significant divisions on the left and the right undermined the legitimacy of leaders of the BPC as the true spokespersons for Bougainville.

Accordingly, there were strong pressures on the leaders of both sides to compromise, and beginning in August 1999 some discussions had been initiated between them. Then, unexpectedly, late in 1999 a PNG court ruled that the suspension by the PNG government of the provincial government structures for Bougainville in January 1999 had been contrary to the PNG constitution. This ruling provided the opportunity for a compromise, and early in December 1999 an agreement was signed between the previously opposing factions under which the BPC accepted the restored provincial government with Momis as governor, while Momis agreed that the provincial government (the Bougainville Interim Provincial Government—BIPG) would govern in full consultation with the BPC.[28] These arrangements operated from late 1999 until the Autonomous Bougainville Government established under the Bougainville Peace Agreement was elected in mid-2005. As a result of this compromise, a united Bougainville leadership (other than Ona and his supporters) adopted a common Bougainville negotiating position and jointly negotiated the political settlement with PNG (as discussed further in this chapter).

Why a Locally Initiated and Controlled Process? Some Key Dynamics

Seven key aspects of the internal dynamics of the peace process are highlighted here as significant in explaining both the development of a locally initiated peace process and the ability of local actors to largely maintain control of it. In the process, local actors felt strongly that for the most part, they were in control of the process.

As a result, although there was a significant international intervention that might have been expected to have strong interests in having some degree of control of the process, local actors were clear that the intervention was put in place at their request. In general, the Bougainville and PNG parties were remarkably tolerant of the presence and the roles played by the international community for two main reasons. First, the parties were very conscious that they needed an international intervention and that without this the tentative and "shaky" process begun earlier would not have, in fact, gotten off the ground. Second, parties to the

28. For more detail of the internal political struggles among the factions supporting the peace process, see Regan, "Why a Neutral Peace Monitoring Force," 12–14.

process felt largely in control of proceedings. At times any particular party might feel that some part of the international intervention was not acting as wanted, but overall there was a high degree of tolerance for the intervention, even when it occasionally did play more activist roles than might have been expected. In addition, of course, the approach that the international intervention itself took to dealing with the parties is a significant factor in explaining both the degree of control maintained by local actors and their tolerance of the activities of the international intervention, issues discussed in the next section of this monograph.

Local Reconciliation and Peacebuilding

As discussed earlier in this chapter ("The 'Informal' Peace Process—Local Reconciliation and Peacebuilding"), the significant participation in reconciliation and peacebuilding efforts by a wide range of leaders in communities in most parts of Bougainville laid the foundations for the peace process. In addition, that broad community engagement in the origins of the process contributed to continued engagement once the process was under way. Local leaders took ownership of the process and were committed to it.

Taking Account of Divisions

As discussed already, concern about the impact on Bougainville of the divisiveness of the conflict was a major factor influencing moderate Bougainvillean leadership of all factions to explore the possibilities of peace. As a result, it was Bougainville leaders, in both 1995 and 1997, who took the initiative in seeking to engage, although they did so with international facilitation (Australia in the 1995 Cairns talks and New Zealand in 1997). Then, once the peace process was under way, there were continuing problems with further fracturing of factions on both the left and the right, putting great pressure on the process. Outcomes included creative efforts to find workable compromises that included arrangements for inclusion of representatives of as many factions as possible in all major negotiation sessions, inclusive of the more than 20 often extended sessions in which the detail of the Bougainville Peace Agreement was negotiated (see chapter 5).

Pressures to Negotiate, Room for Moderates

Another important aspect of the dynamics of the process concerns the particular factors that in the first part of 1997 contributed to pressures on each of the three main parties—or coalitions—to the conflict to engage in a negotiated settlement. The main parties (or coalitions) were the PNG government and the two main sets of Bougainvillean factions, namely the secessionists (the BRA and its civilian government—the BIG—and their supporters) and the integrationists (the BRF, the BTG, and various groups supporting them). The pressures for negotiation created room for moderate leadership to come to the fore in each of the three parties.

While the BRA had the upper hand in the conflict, as already discussed, a majority of its leaders joined most BIG leaders in thinking that outright military victory would probably take time and could be achieved only at a terrible cost of divisiveness. For leaders of the Bougainville factions supporting or sympathetic to PNG, there was also deep concern about divisive impacts of the conflict, growing awareness that the PNG forces were increasingly unlikely to prevail, and general concern about escalating casualty rates (deaths, injuries, and trauma), destruction of the economic base, and so on. At the same time, leaders of all Bougainville factions were under slowly increasing pressure from the growing local mediation and reconciliation efforts already discussed, and from the war weariness of the general population.

As for the PNG government, from the beginning of the conflict significant elements among both political and civil service leaders had supported a peaceful settlement. In 1992 a prime minister committed to a military solution in Bougainville came to power and conflict escalated, but without PNG gaining the upper hand. But by the mid-1990s the human and economic costs of the conflict were mounting, and PNG was under increasing international pressure because of widely reported human rights abuses in Bougainville. Pressure for peace grew when a more moderate prime minister took power in mid-1994, ironically the same Sir Julius Chan who, frustrated with his inability to resolve the Bougainville conflict peacefully, renewed the reliance on military efforts in 1996, and when that failed, sought to engage the Sandline mercenaries in 1997. With widespread recognition that options for PNG were just about exhausted, the way was opened for moderates (in terms of Bougainville policy) to take the upper hand in the PNG government.

The moderate leadership was able to maintain its dominance on all sides, although not without difficulty. Among the Bougainvillean groups, Ona sought to reassert himself against Kabui in the latter half of 1997. However, BRA leaders supporting the embryonic peace process came to the fore at a meeting in Roreinang, in central Bougainville (see Map 6), in September 1997, making it clear that they would not accept action directed at undermining the process. Ona subsequently attempted to orchestrate a flow of public support in his direction by organizing meetings of a wide range of leaders in advance of his announcing the Republic of Me'ekamui in April 1998, but by then the TMG was well established and the PNG government had agreed to a UN observer mission; hope in the peace process was beginning to consolidate. The Bougainvillean pro-integration leaders, who during 1998–99 had split from the cross-factional coalition of moderate leaders that established the BPC, probably expected most pro-integration elements to join them. But when many remained with the BPC, the pressure for a compromise increased. On the PNG side, there was sometimes pressure from radical elements to take a strong stand against any possible concession to Bougainville. But the failure of the attempt to use the Sandline mercenaries to achieve military victory had led most PNG leaders to accept that the military option was no longer viable. Hence, the lack of a realistic alternative to a negotiated settlement was a major factor in favor of the moderates.

While the parties were committed to the peace process, the extent of divisions and mistrust between the parties, already discussed, made progress slow. For example, Ona's opposition was one of many factors that made BRA/BIG leaders supporting the peace process concerned about the danger of losing their support base and encouraged them to continue to push strongly for agreement to early secession in the initial stages of the peace process. Reaching substantial agreement on a final political agreement took a good deal of time.

Wide-Ranging Representation in Negotiations

A fourth aspect of the dynamics involves some of the more significant reasons for the ongoing local support in Bougainville for the process as it unfolded. Bougainvillean leaders had learned important lessons from the experience of negotiations earlier in the 1990s that had mainly involved only senior BRA and BIG leaders. Those leaders had subsequently experienced difficulties in "selling" outcomes to combatant groups and wider communities. In order to avoid any repetition of this experience, a key feature of the first negotiations in New Zealand in mid-1997 (and continued thereafter) was to include in all peace process talks local leaders of the community-based fighting units, which represented both the BRA and the BRF. This meant large numbers of people attending most talks—almost 100 Bougainvilleans went to the first Burnham talks.

Negotiating teams working on the Bougainville Peace Agreement also were widely representative, resulting in teams of 30 or more. New Zealand and Australia at times attempted to limit numbers in order to reduce costs and logistical pressures, but were for the most part persuaded by the Bougainville leaders that the local political and cultural context made inclusiveness vital. One result was that unlike earlier talks, locally based leaders of combatant units understood and felt committed to the agreed outcomes. In turn, they promoted awareness of and support for the process and its outcomes when they returned to their units and communities.

Not surprisingly, the PNG government followed a similar approach to negotiations, taking care to include representatives of a wide range of agencies in negotiating teams. Further, as the political negotiations got under way, a bipartisan parliamentary committee was established involving both government and opposition members of parliament. The committee played a significant consultative role in support of the successive PNG ministers responsible for negotiating a political settlement. These and similar efforts helped to maintain coherence among the disparate parts of the national government and build bipartisan support for negotiated outcomes.

Wariness by the Parties of the International Intervention

From earlier negotiations, parties involved also had experience dealing with the international community, from which they understood some of the risks involved in international interventions. These experiences had taught the PNG government to be extremely wary of such interventions and the BIG/BRA, in particular, to ensure that it was treated as a partner along with the PNG government and the international actors involved. A few examples will suffice to illustrate this point.

On the PNG side, the government was uncertain about the degree that the parties to the international intervention understood the situation and about possible partisanship in favor of Bougainville separatists by some international organizations and especially by the United Nations. The key national government officials involved from 1997 were unaware of the sobering impact on BRA/BIG figures of the UN official who had attended the October 1994 peace conference in Bougainville. Rather, there was concern that UN and Commonwealth Secretariat involvement in the talks among the Bougainville factions in Cairns, in late 1995, may have encouraged BIG/BRA leaders to feel that they were gaining international support for their cause, or that there was international recognition of a right to secede. Such concerns resulted in considerable reluctance to accept the involvement of a UN observer mission in the process that began mid-1997. Even when PNG had reluctantly conceded the need for involvement of the international community in the peace process, the government pressed to ensure that the roles of international parties be strictly limited, in particular, the UN and the PMG.

On the BIG/BRA side, continuing resentment simmered that PNG had failed to involve their leaders in negotiation of arrangements for the SPPKF in advance of the October 1994 peace conference in Arawa, Bougainville.[29] BIG/BRA representatives, therefore, insisted that the Burnham Truce of October 1997 provide for full consultation with the Bougainville parties, and that Bougainville be a party to any status of forces agreement in relation to the peacekeeping force envisaged by that document.[30]

Suspicion of Australia

The sixth aspect of the dynamics of the process (closely related to the preceding one) concerns a degree of suspicion of—even some hostility—on the part of the parties toward some participants in the interna-

29. Breen, *Giving Peace a Chance*, 58–60.

30. Regan, "Establishing the Truce Monitoring Group," 23–25.

tional intervention, specifically Australian negotiators and the Australian military. Such attitudes did not necessarily outweigh awareness of the need for assistance from the international community if the peace process was to succeed, but did contribute to a strong motivation to limit the degree of control over the process exercised by any "suspect" participant in the intervention.

Suspicion toward Australia came from not only Bougainville groups—especially the BIG/BRA leadership—but also from many in the PNG government. In addition, some saw New Zealand as too close to Australia.[31] A major factor here was the fact that many Bougainvilleans held Australia responsible for the conflict because it imposed the Panguna mine as a colonial ruler. Because BCL's majority shareholder (Conzinc Riotinto Australia Ltd) was an Australia-registered company, many Bougainvilleans regarded BCL as an Australian entity (though, in fact, the Australian government did not own shares in either BCL or its parent company). Australia had played important roles facilitating Bougainville peace efforts before 1997, and indeed from at least 1993 applied pressure on PNG to work toward a peaceful resolution of the conflict.[32] However, the perception among Bougainvilleans was that it had taken sides, actively supporting PNG. In particular, there was strong resentment about Australia's role in supplying and training PNG forces during the conflict (mainly—but not only—under longstanding bilateral arrangements). The equipment supplied had included military helicopters, which the PNGDF had used as gunships in both combat with the BRA and in operations in which it was widely reported that Bougainvillean civilians were targeted. Further, until 1996 Australian policy had prohibited its politicians and civil servants from engaging with BRA and BIG representatives. By contrast, the sensitivity toward Australia among certain elements in the PNG government was (ironically) in part due to the perception that Australia had not provided sufficient support to the PNG forces during the conflict and in part due to Australia's strong public opposition to the use of the Sandline mercenaries early in 1997.

31. See, for example, Siara, "The Time Is Now," 127–28.

32. Ibid.

PNG Concerns about Sovereignty and Secession

One of the chief concerns of the government of PNG was that the peace process be managed in a way to reduce the risk that Bougainville would secede. As a relatively new independent country made up of an incredible diversity of peoples, PNG officials were driven by a strong sense of nationalism and were deeply concerned that secession could undermine the new country's unity and become a precedent for other parts of the still-fragile nation.[33] In addition, the moderate political leadership that took control of the government after mid-1997 recognized that government policies had contributed significantly to prolonging the conflict. These officials felt that negotiation was the best method to end years of civil strife and that both the PNG and Bougainville officials, representing Melanesian societies, could do so by controlling the process. This strong sentiment was a factor in the in PNG government negotiations with parties sometimes arguing for limited roles for not only the UN and the PMG, but also foreign advisers to the Bougainville leaders. Such arguments were a source of tension, as the Bougainvillean leadership in general supported expansive roles for the international intervention, and strongly opposed any suggestion of interference by the national government in relation to the sources of advice utilized by Bougainville. Nevertheless, the national government attitude did result in some pressure for limiting the role of the intervention.

Management of the Process by the Parties

While the main parties (BRA/BIG, BRF/BTG, and the PNG government) had to take into account several significant difficulties in developing arrangements for management of the peace process, they were ultimately successful in establishing and operating an adaptable framework of institutions and relationships for that purpose.

33. PNG had experienced a number of "micronationalist" movements in the period before and just after independence, several of which espoused separatist sentiments. See Ronald May, ed., *Micronationalist Movements in Papua New Guinea* (Canberra: Australian National University, 1982).

Difficulties Taken into Account

Three major sets of difficulties had to be considered: First, the Bougainville factions were not integrated and structured organizations, but rather, and for the most part, loose coalitions of locally based groups. Second, the PNG government was not monolithic, but rather a set of disparate organizations with different agendas and goals. Finally, the parties were extremely suspicious of one another and initially had great difficulty in working together.

During talks, the Bougainville groups dealt with their lack of integration by generally taking an extremely inclusive approach to all public activities, whether political or peace process related. The reconciliation government (the BPC) established in May 1998 was large (about 110 members), its composition mainly elected but also partly appointed, to ensure as many groups as possible had a voice. The locally based former combatant groups were given some representation in the political structures, as well as in most aspects of the peace process, inclusive of the negotiations, as already discussed. There was constant consultation among the leaders of the political groupings and the leadership of the former combatants.

The PNG government made similar efforts to constantly consult. Among political leaders in the cabinet and the legislature, ongoing efforts from the time the peace process had begun ensured that Bougainville was treated as a bipartisan issue, an approach that successive governments have adhered to from 1997 to the present. It was often more difficult to ensure integration of and cooperation among government departments and institutions, but with strong political support for the peace process, there was pressure on even dissenting elements of the bureaucracy to conform. Strong leadership by successive chief secretaries (the name for the position of head of the Department of Prime Minister and National Executive Council) and a coordinating role played by an Office of Bougainville Affairs based in the chief secretary's department have also helped to maintain a reasonable degree of coherence on the part of the PNG government during negotiations and also in subsequent implementation phases.

The suspicions between the parties (between not only opposing Bougainville parties, but also Bougainville secessionists and PNG) were not easily dealt with. Of critical importance here was the role of the international intervention in terms of creating a secure space within which the parties could engage and begin to work together, as discussed in chapter 4.

An Adaptable Framework for Management of the Process by the Parties

Together the parties gradually developed a framework of institutions and relationships through which they managed and made decisions about the peace process, though their decisions and actions were often influenced, to varying degrees, by one aspect or another of the international intervention. That framework emerged through a series of ad hoc decisions and gradual development of practice rather than through any grand plan and included

- Major meetings between the parties, such as those early meetings in New Zealand, to agree to the road map of steps in the process and later meetings in PNG where agreements were negotiated or signed.
- Consultative and decisionmaking mechanisms involving all parties, notably in the shape of one body of central importance, namely the Peace Process Consultative Committee (PPCC), to represent not only the parties to the ceasefire but also the UN mission and the PMG, chaired mainly by the director of the UN mission.
- The PPCC to deal initially with truce and ceasefire monitoring reports from the TMG and PMG and subsequently gradually also take on problem-solving and goal-setting roles, including oversight of aspects of UN-supervised disarmament process (below).
- Ad hoc meetings of two or more of the parties to deal with particular issues and problems, something that occurred with increasing frequency as trust between the parties grew.
- Both direct and indirect communication between the parties, initially often facilitated by the regional truce and ceasefire monitoring groups and the UN observer mission, but increasingly a matter of direct communication as trust grew.

- More than twenty direct meetings of officials and advisers and also political leaders between June 1999 and August 2001 to negotiate the Bougainville Peace Agreement.

The one potentially important institution that was not controlled by both parties was the Peace Process Steering Committee (PPSC), comprising the PMG commander and representatives of the four countries contributing to the PMG. The PPSC was intended as a consultative body that enabled the contributing countries to consider progress of the PMG and any adjustments that might need to be made (its role is touched upon further in chapter 4).

4

The International Intervention and Its Relationship to Local Actors

Involvement by international parties during the peace process was at the behest of and operated within parameters set by the PNG government or Bougainville entities. More important, international actors managed their support carefully and sensitively, partly because of past experience in dealing with the Bougainville conflict, and partly because the key actors in the intervention were well aware of local concerns regarding both PNG's and Bougainville's past experience with Australian interests.[1]

Overview of Main Elements of the Intervention

While the most visible elements of the intervention were the regional truce and ceasefire monitoring missions (the TMG and the PMG) and the UN observer mission, other important elements also played significant roles.

---

1. For a discussion of key issues concerning the design and operation of the international intervention, see Joseph Kabui, "Reconciliation A Priori"; John Hayes, "Bringing Peace to Bougainville"; and Anthony J. Regan, "The Bougainville Intervention: Political Legitimacy and Sustainable Peace-Building," in Greg Fry and Tarcisius Kabutaulaka, eds., *Intervention and State-Building in the Pacific: The Legitimacy of "Cooperative Intervention"* (Manchester: Manchester University Press, 2008), 184–208. For a discussion of the TMG and the PMG, see Roger Mortlock, "A Good Thing to Do"; Roger Mortlock, "Lessons from Bougainville"; Wehner and Denoon, *Without a Gun;* Bob Breen, "Reflections on the Truce Monitoring Group," in Garasu and Carl, eds., *Weaving Consensus*, 56–57; and Natascha Spark and Jackie Bailey, "Disarmament in Bougainville: 'Guns in Boxes,'" *International Peacekeeping* 12, no. 4 (2005), 599–608. For a discussion of the UN observer mission, see Scott Smith, "The Role of the United Nations Observer Mission," in Garasu and Carl, eds., *Weaving Consensus*, 54–55. For a discussion of PNG government perspectives on developing and managing the international intervention, see Edward P. Wolfers, "International Peace Missions in Bougainville, Papua New Guinea, 1990–2005: Host State Perceptions," paper presented to the Regional Forum on Reinventing Government: Exchange and Transfer of Innovations for Transparent Governance and State Capacity, Nadi, Fiji, February 20–22, 2006.

Activities Necessary to Establish and Maintain the Intervention

Among the activities needed to establish and maintain the intervention were significant facilitation, support, and mediation roles played mainly by senior diplomats from New Zealand, Australia, and Solomon Islands. In the early stages they helped to encourage leaders of the parties to engage—and remain engaged—in the process. Solomon Islands leaders also played key chairing roles at some of the early meetings in New Zealand.

New Zealand and Australia played major facilitation roles throughout the process. In later stages, during the negotiation of the political agreement and the initial steps in its implementation, the Australian and New Zealand foreign ministers, and more particularly their ambassadors to PNG, played significant mediating, encouraging, and cajoling roles. Another element of the intervention closely linked to the facilitation and mediation roles played by New Zealand and Australia involved hosting meetings of leaders or advisers and officials of the parties, mainly in the early stages of the process when distrust among the parties and concerns about security ruled out meetings in Bougainville or elsewhere in PNG. New Zealand hosted the major officials and political talks—Burnham in July 1997, Burnham again in October 1997, and Lincoln in January 1998. Australia hosted officials talks in Cairns in November 1997 and in Canberra in March 1998 and also a major meeting later in the process, in February 2001 when it brought over 100 BRA and BRF commanders to Townsville to try to reach agreement on a disarmament process (see Map 1 for the locations of these talks).

Both Australia and New Zealand, as well as the UNDP, provided significant levels of funding for a range of activities beyond just facilitation of meetings and negotiations, including awareness programs for their various key constituents by Bougainville leaders after key rounds of negotiations or in support of implementation of parts of the Bougainville Peace Agreement (for example, awareness about disarmament arrangements or the autonomy arrangements, both of which are described later). Australia also funded key technical advisers to each of the main parties—PNG, BRA/BIG, and BTG/BRF. There was also support for implementation of the disarmament process and reintegration of former combatants through funding of small projects; support for a two-year consultative process (2002–4) to forge a constitution for an autonomous Bougainville government; technical support for elections for the Autonomous Bougainville Government (ABG) held in mid-2005; and from mid-2005 technical and advisory support to the administrative arm of the ABG in relation to ongoing implementation of the autonomy arrangements under the peace agreement.

The Regional Truce and Ceasefire Monitoring Groups, December 1997 to June 2003

The unarmed regional truce and cease-fire monitoring groups—the New Zealand–led Truce Monitoring Group that monitored the truce from 1997 to April 1998 and the Australian-led Peace Monitoring Group that monitored the ceasefire from its inception in May 1998 until mid-2003—comprised personnel from four countries, namely New Zealand, Australia, Fiji, and Vanuatu.[2] These were not just the most visible elements of the intervention, but also the most complex and expensive. At its largest, the PMG involved over 300 personnel (reduced to 75 in the months just before its departure), operating from as many as seven different sites in various parts of Bougainville (see Map 6), namely a logistical support base at the former mining company seaport at Loloho and five monitoring team sites and a "forward support base." The public face of the PMG (and the TMG before it) was its monitoring teams (based in Arawa, Buka Town, Buin Town, Wakunai, and Tonu, and a "forward support base" for the Tonu monitoring team site at Sirakatau), which patrolled constantly in the villages and hamlets in the areas for which they were responsible (see map 6). Under agreements between PNG and the four contributing countries, the Australian and New Zealand governments led, funded, and provided most personnel and logistical support for both the TMG and the PMG. Because of the sensitivity that some in the Bougainville leadership had shown about Australian military support to PNG during the conflict, the numerous military personnel from Australia who were part of the TMG and (especially) the PMG played solely logistical and support roles, with civilians

2. The PMG operated under a "Protocol" to the agreement of December 5, 1997, that had provided for the establishment and operation of the TMG. The full text of the "Protocol" is reproduced as appendix E in Wehner and Denoon, *Without a Gun*, 178–84.

(officials from public service departments) being the only Australian members of the monitoring teams. By contrast, it was security force personnel from New Zealand, Fiji, and Vanuatu who were supplied as the monitors (of the truce or ceasefire, as the case may be). It was generally New Zealand and in some cases Fijian military personnel who were the officers in charge of the monitoring teams and so were most often required to undertake sensitive duties, such as investigating alleged truce or ceasefire breaches. TMG and PMG personnel received extensive training before they were posted to Bougainville, with those assigned to be monitors in particular receiving training in history, cultural awareness, and negotiation skills, which emphasized the need to be patient and to use a nonconfrontational approach when dealing with not only combatants but with the Bougainville population generally, so many of whom had been severely traumatized by the conflict.

Personnel from Fiji and Vanuatu were originally included in the TMG and PMG largely because of the interest by Australian and New Zealand planners in the enhanced legitimacy expected if the TMG and PMG were to be seen as involving representatives of Pacific island countries, making the peace process a truly regional enterprise.[3] In practice, these monitoring team members were found to be invaluable, particularly because of their ability to understand Bougainville culture and to often achieve rapport with Bougainvilleans far more quickly than the New Zealand or Australian personnel. Vanuatu personnel also had significant advantages in terms of language skills—the Vanuatu lingua franca (Bislama) is very similar to that of PNG, including Bougainville (Melanesian Tok Pisin). Despite these advantages, there were some difficulties integrating some of the Vanuatu and Fiji personnel into the monitoring teams that were predominantly made up of Australian and New Zealand personnel.[4]

It must be emphasized that these significant contributions to the intervention (that is, the TMG and PMG) were specifically requested by the parties to the process and not imposed in any way by the international community. In the case of the TMG, this was achieved through agreements reached by the parties in Burnham in October 1997 and at

3. Regan, "The Bougainville Intervention."

4. See Breen, "Reflections on the Truce Monitoring Group," 56.

a meeting of officials in Cairns in November 1997.[5] The request for the PMG was contained in an annex to the Lincoln Agreement signed on April 30, 1998, which contained the terms of the ceasefire.[6] Further, for reasons already touched on, the Bougainville parties insisted that they be involved in all main decisions about the roles and rules covering the TMG and the PMG.[7]

The main official responsibility of the TMG and PMG involved monitoring the truce and the subsequent cease-fire respectively, and this required investigating and reporting to the parties about alleged breaches of the truce or ceasefire. In addition, their responsibilities included keeping the Bougainville community informed about the peace process (through regular patrols, newsletters, and other means), facilitating the peace process in a range of ways (transport of leaders to meetings, for instance), and mediating some issues dividing parties or factions. Beginning in 2001, the PMG also provided extensive technical and logistical support with implementation of the disarmament process supervised by the UN mission.[8] (The provision for that process in the Bougainville Peace Agreement and its implementation are discussed in chapter 5).

The small monitoring teams that were the public face of the TMG and PMG were supported by a main base at Loloho, near Arawa in central Bougainville, providing communications, helicopter support, logistics, medical support, and so forth. Large numbers of logistical and support personnel were needed, especially for the TMG and the early stages of the PMG, because the Bougainville terrain is very rugged, roads had not been maintained for many years, telecommunication facilities had been destroyed, recent violent conflict meant very little

5. See the Burnham Truce, paragraph 6 (www.c-r.org/our-work/accord/png-bougainville/key-texts15.php), and the Cairns Commitment (www.c-r.org/our-work/accord/png-bougainville/key-texts17.php).

6. This was the Arawa Agreement (Agreement Covering Implementation of the Ceasefire), the full text of which can be found at www.c-r.org/our-work/accord/png-bougainville/key-texts21.php (accessed August 10, 2009).

7. For a more detailed discussion of the origins of and negotiation and operation of the agreements concerning the TMG and the PMG, see Kabui, "Reconciliation A Priori"; Mortlock, "A Good Thing to Do"; and Regan, "Establishing the Truce Monitoring Group."

8. Spark and Bailey, "Disarmament in Bougainville."

freedom of movement, and no fundamental services were available in most areas, such as basic health care. So TMG and PMG needed to supply its own needs, as well as assist the leadership of the Bougainville factions with transport, security, communications, and even health care. Transport needs alone were considerable, including numerous four-wheel-drive vehicles and several helicopters to cover the terrain.

While both TMG and PMG were led by military representatives, civilians played significant roles. In particular, the effective second-in-command was always an Australian civilian occupying a position known as the "chief negotiator," indicating an intended division of responsibility between a military manager of the whole operation and a civilian who handled more politically delicate dealings with leaders of Bougainville factions, PNG forces and the government, and others. Especially in the first two years, the chief negotiators were senior officials with extensive experience in Bougainville, PNG, and the wider Pacific. The intended division of responsibility did not always work well, with some military commanders seeking to get heavily involved in dealing with the parties, sometimes, in part, in response to pressure from the Australian Department of Defense and senior Australian Army authorities who were focused on achieving an early exit date and also felt that the UN observer mission, in particular, was not being sufficiently proactive in encouraging the progress of the peace process (a matter discussed further below).

The decision that the TMG should be unarmed—largely based on Bougainvillean concerns that Ona and other peace process opponents would misinterpret deployment of an armed group—was one with which many in the Australian Army and Department of Defense were never entirely comfortable. In fact it was a position agreed to only after intense debate within the Australian bureaucracy, with the Department of Foreign Affairs and Trade eventually prevailing over the concerns of the defense department. An unarmed body was seen as contrary to entrenched views about the role of a military force and also raised concerns about force security in what was seen as a dangerously unstable situation, especially in the early stages when Francis Ona's intentions were unclear. However, unintended but positive consequences of the arrangement included the ability of unarmed monitors to challenge the notions of Bougainvillean combatants about the roles of warriors, demonstrating that soldiers could work for peace in a peaceful manner. An additional significant factor here was the inclusion of female personnel among the TMG and PMG monitoring teams (military personnel from New Zealand, Fiji, and Vanuatu, and civilians from Australia), again challenging ideas about the roles of warriors. Being unarmed also reinforced the light footprint approach of the intervention and encouraged the TMG and the PMG to put great emphasis on building good relations with all parties and with the Bougainvillean communities more generally. Consequently, responsibility for protection of the security of members of the TMG and the PMG was in the hands of combatant groups. Ironically, the highly visible presence of women monitors was a factor here, for in matrilineal Bougainville the role of men in protecting women (the source of the members of the clans) is taken very seriously, and BRA and BRF personnel clearly took seriously the responsibility of ensuring the safety of the female monitors.[9]

In practice, the decision for both the TMG and the PMG to be unarmed worked remarkably well. One measure of success was the fact that no TMG or PMG member was seriously injured or killed when on duty[10]—although there were a few isolated incidents where personnel in PMG vehicles were fired at, probably by MDF elements. As already discussed, success also flowed in large part because both BRA and BRF leaders had reached the conclusion that a military victory would be too difficult and divisive to achieve and, as a result, were themselves opposed to the use of weapons to undermine the peace process. Further, the assessment of the BRA and BIG leaders who advised the Resource Group preparing proposals for the TMG between October and November 1997 was that although BRA elements then supporting Ona (later to become MDF) carried weapons and might oppose the peace process, they were scattered and militarily weak when compared to the preponderance of BRA elements that supported the peace process. That analysis was to remain valid throughout the process. Finally, it was widely believed in Bougainville that although the TMG and PMG did

9. I am grateful to David Hallett, the last chief negotiator for the PMG, for drawing this point to my attention.

10. One PMG member died, but it was in the course of recreational diving.

not have weapons "on the ground," they almost certainly could get access to weapons quickly should there be a real threat to their personnel. In particular, the Australians were believed to have weapons available on naval vessels almost always anchored offshore from their main base at Loloho.

Throughout the time the PMG operated, there was a struggle within the Australian bureaucracy about when it should leave, with the Army and the Department of Defense always seeking the earliest possible exit date, and the Department of Foreign Affairs and Trade and Department of Prime Minister and Cabinet generally supporting the need for a more extended presence. By 2002, however, even the latter departments were beginning to support the need for departure of the PMG, because of signs that the Bougainville leadership was growing ever more dependent on the PMG for, among other things, transport, mediation, and weapons disposal. There was consensus in the relevant parts of the Australian bureaucracy about the need for Bougainvilleans to find ways of dealing with their own problems, to take more responsibility for the whole peace process, without always relying on the PMG and the UN mission.[11]

Ultimately the PMG ceased operating on June 30, 2003, very much against the wishes of Bougainville leaders, who appealed the decision a number of times to the Australian government. They were concerned on several fronts. In particular, Ona, his Me'ekamui government, and the MDF all remained outside the peace process. The MDF, holding several hundred weapons, was not participating in the agreed disarmament process under the Bougainville Peace Agreement, and it was widely believed that at least one key MDF commander had been actively involved in late 2002 and early 2003 in thefts of BRA and BRF weapons previously contained as part of the disarmament process. Further, that process was, in any event, only partially complete in June 2003, and the PMG had been playing major roles in providing logistical and technical support that had been vital to the progress of containment of weapons up to that point. The Bougainville leaders argued that in these circumstances the peace process could be at risk if the PMG were to leave.

11. I am grateful to David Hallett for drawing my attention to this fact.

In general, however, regional capitals (especially in Australia and New Zealand) believed that the peace process had become well embedded by mid-2003, and that the PMG's departure did not involve significant risks.

The Bougainville Transitional Team, 2003

Before the disbanding of the PMG in June, however, and under pressure from some Bougainville leaders as well as its own concerns with possible risks of removing the PMG, the Australian government proposed in April a compromise: the Bougainville Transitional Team, a group of 13 civilians, based at Arawa and Buka Town, to help maintain confidence in the peace process. Its formal mandate was to assist in facilitating the peace process and to provide support to the Bougainville administration. It operated for six months, July to December 2003.

The UN Monitoring Mission, August 1998 to June 2005

If the TMG and the PMG were the most visible aspects of the intervention, the United Nations monitoring mission that began operating in Arawa, Bougainville, in August 1998 was the most sensitive. It was a tiny operation, comprising only six personnel supplied by the UN and a few locally engaged support staff. Only three of the UN staff played public monitoring roles, with others in support roles. From 1998 to 2003 it was known officially (in the UN system) as the United Nations Political Office in Bougainville (UNPOB). The name reflected its nature as a "political office" under the UN's Department of Political Affairs (UN-DPA), rather than a UN peacekeeping operation established under its Department of Peace Keeping Operations (UN-DPKO). For the PNG government, however, the notion of a UN political office was itself sensitive (the fear being that it might suggest to the BRA/BIG leadership that a political office involved some element of recognition of a right to self-determination), while the agreed observer mission status was acceptable. Hence, in PNG the mission was known as the UN Observer Mission Bougainville (UNOMB). In due course, from 2004 to 2005, the official name within the UN system was, in fact, changed to UNOMB, mainly with a view to suggesting a changed mandate in a situation where the UN-DPA was experiencing some difficulty in persuading the General Assembly to fund an extension of the mission's mandate.

The UN office's original official mandate, agreed to among the UN, PNG, and the Bougainville leaders, was to monitor the ceasefire and chair the main body, the Peace Process Consultative Committee, through which the parties monitored and made decisions about the peace process. In addition, its role was generally understood to extend to monitoring other aspects of the peace process, inclusive of the performance of the PMG. The UN mission also developed a number of additional roles in various ways connected with its original mandate or undertaken by request of the parties. These included facilitating aspects of the peace process (transporting leaders to meetings, for instance) and, from June 1999, chairing most of the negotiations for the Bougainville Peace Agreement, while at the same time also playing a key role in mediating some major divisive issues during those negotiations, and encouraging the parties and factions to remain committed to the process.

Beginning in 1999 the official mandate was expanded by a PPCC request to develop a plan for disarmament by the former combatants. Under the ultimate plan, included in the Bougainville Peace Agreement, the mission was vested with responsibility to coordinate its implementation. From late 2001 until its departure in June 2005, the mission played a significant role in encouraging BRA and BRF members to first place weapons in secure containment and then (mainly from 2004) to destroy them. In the period until the PMG's departure in June 2003, the UN worked closely with the PMG to design and implement the containment phase, with the PMG carrying out the major part of the technical and logistical work involved in providing secure storage of weapons.

The idea of UN involvement in the peace process had been central to most BRA/BIG peace proposals since the early 1990s, and the Burnham Declaration specifically included the UN in its demand for "a neutral peacekeeping force . . . under the auspices of the United Nations."[12] While BRA/BIG leaders had always hoped that UN involvement would help their cause, by 1997 most of them were well aware that such involvement would not be tantamount to international recognition of a

12. Burnham Declaration, paragraph 5.1.

right to secede. In fact, a more important consideration involved concerns that any regional monitoring body might be too heavily dominated by Australia, and UN involvement was seen as an important way of ensuring the neutrality of the regional mission.

It was, of course, the PNG government that was highly sensitive about the UN mission. Senior officers in the PNG bureaucracy as well as some political leaders were strongly opposed to the idea, seeing it as likely to "internationalize" the process and result in a hardening of separatist positions. However, the moderate (in terms of Bougainville issues) political leadership of PNG that supported initiation of the peace process in July 1997 was willing to consider the possibility of UN involvement. In the lead-up to the first negotiations between political leaders from PNG and Bougainville at Lincoln (New Zealand) in January 1998, it was clear that the BRA/BIG proposal for a UN role was going to be a major agenda issue. And it was only very shortly before the talks began that a consensus emerged in the PNG delegation around the proposal to include the UN. The BRA/BIG leadership had been applying considerable pressure, indicating that their participation in the Lincoln talks was dependent on agreement on UN involvement in the peace process. However, PNG officials have since indicated that while pressure was a factor, the critical thing was the willingness of the new political leadership to try new approaches to achieving a peaceful resolution of the conflict. There was an additional factor involved, too: the proposed UN role would subject the resented Australian involvement in the PMG to monitoring, and this made the overall approach more readily acceptable to PNG.

From the early 1990s, the main senior UN official maintaining interest in and links with Bougainville had been Francisc Vendrell in the UN-DPA. Largely because of this, that department staffed the monitoring mission rather than the UN-DPKO, through which the vast majority of UN peacekeeping and peace-monitoring missions is provided. This fact had two significant consequences. First, it meant that finding UN funding for the mission could be problematic; unlike the UN-DPKO, the UN-DPA did not budget for such operations. As a result, the mission was often under threat because of uncertainty about funding, leading to its mandate being extended on several occasions by relatively short periods. Second, as a UN-DPA mission, the Bougainville monitoring mission was probably more flexible than most UN-DPKO missions, which tend to be run on the basis of a well-established, even formulaic, approach.

That the mission approached its duties flexibly was also in large part a result of the leadership of Noel Sinclair, who directed the mission from 1999 to 2003. Sinclair was the former UN ambassador of Guyana, and, in terms of flexibility, it was an advantage that he was not a UN career officer steeped in UN procedures. Further, by remaining in the post for such an extended period, he developed a good understanding of the local cultural and political context. He understood the need to consult widely and to develop broad consensus. In the process of carrying out the mission's official mandate as well as the additional roles it developed, as outlined above, both Sinclair and his successor (UN career officer Thor Stenbock) worked hard to remain in good communication with all factions and parties. This included Francis Ona and his Me'ekamui government, with which Sinclair met several times, with a view to minimizing the possibility of tensions and misunderstandings occurring that might undermine the process.

The main official role of the UN mission involved monitoring the peace process as a whole, inclusive of the operation of the PMG. Once the mission was on the ground (in mid-1998, more than a year after the first Burnham talks), it gradually took over responsibility from the PMG for dealing with the political aspects of the peace process, including negotiations and mediation. It was then in a stronger position than the PMG to influence the agenda, sequencing, and pace of the process.

At times there were tensions between the PMG and the UN mission, with the PMG leadership responding to pressure from senior Australian army and Department of Defense officials seeking rapid progress in the process to enable a quick exit. The PMG leadership, as well as officials in the Australian embassy in PNG, sometimes felt that the UN mission, especially under Noel Sinclair, was simply too relaxed and not doing enough to encourage the parties to resolve issues and move ahead. In general, however, key Bougainvilleans saw the approach pursued by Sinclair as generally appropriate, largely as a result of his sensitivity to and knowledge of the situation gained through his extended period of service in Bougainville. By contrast, even the most senior PMG personnel undertook tours of duty of just a few months at a time, a few (though by no means all) seeming to be more concerned with responding to pressures from the Australian authorities than in gaining a deep understanding of the extent of the obstacles to sustainable peace.

Humanitarian and Development Assistance

A number of countries and entities—especially Australia, New Zealand, the European Union, the International Committee of the Red Cross, the United Nations Development Program (UNDP), and international NGOs—funded humanitarian assistance and development aid (activities largely separate from those involved in the donor-country facilitation of the peace process already discussed).[13] In the early stages of the peace process (1997–98), the focus was largely on humanitarian assistance, especially for the internally displaced persons living in "care centers." But there was also funding for small projects (construction of school classrooms, small health facilities, and similar projects), offered often as a "peace dividend" for communities in areas that supported the peace process. Then in 1998–99 the focus moved to promoting economic development. A joint UNDP/Australian Agency for International Development (AusAID) project funded rehabilitation of the cocoa industry, while at the same time a major AusAID project funded rehabilitation of the main coastal trunk road on Bougainville Island and the main wharves used for shipping cargo to and from Bougainville. The road project (an ongoing maintenance component continues at the time of this writing) encouraged and supported local contractors and work gangs hired to do the work, thereby providing employment and business opportunities to former combatants, creating sustainable local construction capacity, and injecting funds into the local economy. Together, the expansion of cocoa production and the opening of the main road and the wharves had begun to have a dramatic impact on

13. For an overview of issues about and modalities of delivery of donor assistance during the Bougainville conflict and in the early part of the peace process (1997–2002), see Julie Eagles, "Aid as an Instrument for Peace: A Civil Society Perspective," in Carl and Garasu, eds., *Weaving Consensus*, 50–53. For a discussion of other aspects of activities of the Australian and New Zealand governments as major donors, see Regan, "The Bougainville Intervention."

economic activity in Bougainville by 2000–1.[14] Achieving these outcomes was supported by a range of other donor inputs, including European Union funding for rehabilitation of networks of local rural roads ("feeder roads").

There has also been funding for a wide range of infrastructure development, inclusive of schools, health services, and the law and justice sector (court rooms, police stations, and other structures). Both New Zealand Aid and AusAID have also given considerable support to "capacity-building" efforts for the Bougainville administration and for the elements of the PNG police working in Bougainville and partially under control of the Autonomous Bougainville Government. This assistance has been in accordance with requests from the leaders of the BTG (and since 2005 the ABG), as well as senior Bougainville administration and police officials.

Virtually all of the various forms of assistance provided by donors have made significant contributions to the restoration of basic services and infrastructure in Bougainville and in support of the peace process. Donor contributions were especially important in the early stages, when the Bougainville administration was particularly weak and the PNG government was restricted from operating in Bougainville. But some difficulties arose with the way donor funding was made available, as discussed later in under "Some Unintended Consequences of Donor Funding Arrangements."

Factors Moderating International Activism

With the funding resources and sufficient personnel, Australia was the only country in the region prepared to participate for the long term during peace negotiations. Further, it had a strong strategic interest in seeing an end to the Bougainville conflict, which it regarded as undermining the unity and stability of PNG and threatening regional stability. As the country with the highest population in the Pacific island community and Australia's nearest neighbor and former colonial territory, PNG is of critical importance to Australian security; any signifi-

14. Ian Scales, Raoul Craemer, and Indra Thappa, *Market Chain Development in Peace Building: Australia's Roads, Wharves and Agriculture Projects in Post-Conflict Bougainville* (Canberra: AusAID, 2008).

cant civil conflict there could contribute to regional instability. New Zealand accepted the need for Australian involvement, acknowledging that both its resources (in terms of funding and military assets) and its status as the major regional power with a long-term close relationship to PNG made Australian cooperation essential. At the same time, Australia accepted that New Zealand was better equipped to take the initial lead in providing such support because of many Bougainvilleans' suspicions surrounding Australia.

In general, the New Zealand and Australian governments, and their respective military and diplomatic arms, cooperated well in the planning and implementation of the TMG. At the same time, this aspect of the process was not without its tensions. At times, New Zealand resentment of its larger, more powerful, and sometimes more insensitive neighbor was evident. New Zealand tends to see itself as far more integrated in and connected with the Pacific islands and their peoples than is Australia. Factors here include New Zealand's large indigenous Maori population, as well as its many immigrants from other Pacific countries. In the context of the Bougainville intervention, many New Zealand civilian and military personnel felt that they were more "culturally sensitive" than their Australian colleagues and made those views quite clear, sometimes causing considerable resentment on the part of Australian personnel. For their part, Australian military planners tended to regard the New Zealand military as poorly equipped, and perhaps not as well organized as their Australian counterparts, and their attitudes tended to be resented on the New Zealand side. Such tensions did not undermine the generally positive cooperation, although they could cause friction. For example, Australian criticisms of New Zealand's limited resourcing of the TMG influenced Australian decisions to ensure that the PMG was larger and better equipped than the TMG in its early stages, contributing to some criticisms from many in the New Zealand system (as well as some Australian civilian planners) who felt that the PMG was too large and expensive to operate effectively, an inappropriate form of organization for the situation.

Adding to the tensions between these two Antipodean powers was that Australian representatives saw New Zealand's initiatives in the early stages of the peace process as involving an attempt to expand into

Australia's sphere of influence in Melanesia (or the southwest Pacific). Countering this view, some New Zealand officials made it clear that their efforts to lead in the regional efforts reflected an interest in playing a more active leadership role in the southwest Pacific.

All parties recognize the reality of New Zealand's neutrality. The country had no prior colonial role in PNG (its links prior to the conflict were largely limited to church contacts and so regarded favorably)[15] and also had limited ongoing military links, and, unlike Australia, it had had no prior policy limiting its contacts with the BRA and BIG. New Zealand Foreign Minister Don McKinnon and senior advisers quickly built trust with both the Bougainvillean parties and PNG figures through preparation for and facilitation of the initial peace talks in New Zealand in July and October 1997 and January 1998, during which they played some important mediating roles. So while there were Australian critics, at the same time the advantages of New Zealand leadership were recognized, but most parties anticipated that Australia would continue to be involved in all events, inclusive of providing funding, personnel, and holding the deputy leadership of the TMG.

Within months, however, the financial and logistical burdens involved in leading and providing most personnel and equipment for the TMG had become too much for New Zealand. Beginning with the establishment of the PMG in May 1998, leadership of the unarmed regional monitoring group passed from New Zealand to Australia. While New Zealand continued to play important roles in the process, its involvement diminished as Australia gradually took on a more active role in the process. However, the PMG leadership managed the situation with an eye to the sensitivities of the parties, so that although the numbers of New Zealand personnel in the PMG were much reduced when compared to the TMG, many of the continuing personnel played major and public roles. They commanded monitoring teams and were part of the small PMG senior leadership team that dealt most directly with the senior Bougainville leadership. In fact, in general, the New Zealand and Fiji personnel tended to play a disproportionately important role in the monitoring teams compared to

15. I am grateful to Stephen Henningham for drawing my attention to this point.

their numbers, whereas most Australian personnel played support roles out of the public eye.[16]

In general, while playing the leading role in terms of international community support for the peace process (from early 1997 to April 1998), New Zealand saw its role as one of facilitating rather than directing the process and, for the most part, recognized the leadership role of the PNG and Bougainvillean parties (the main exception being that on some occasions some senior Bougainvilleans were concerned that one New Zealand diplomat sought to exercise excessive control of the process). While there was some disquiet in the Australian bureaucracy about the slow progress in negotiations during this period, the approach remained the same even once the lead passed to Australia in May 1998, largely due to local suspicion concerning Australian intent and to the consequential dangers for safety of PMG personnel should Australian activism cause local resentment. Accordingly, Australia accepted both that the agenda and the timetable for the peace process needed to be largely determined by the parties to the conflict, and that the PMG should play a supportive and facilitative role, even though many in the Australian system did not really understand why the peace process moved at what, to them, seemed a frustratingly slow pace.

In retrospect, both the tension between Australia and New Zealand and Australia's diffidence about its role contributed to the positive outcomes of the whole process. The tension between the two encouraged each to exercise great care in dealing with the PNG and Bougainville parties to the process, always seeking to avoid any appearance of insensitivity or domination. Concerning Australia's diffidence, had that country sought to play the more expansive and agenda-setting role (directed particularly at accelerating the pace of the process) that some key Australian figures would have preferred, it is likely that considerable resistance to the intervention would have resulted, and the local dynamics that permitted the resolution of tensions and reconciliation of differences would have been stifled. See more on this in chapter 7.

16. Ibid.

Planning and Managing the Intervention—The Internal Aspect

As noted, the early stages of planning for the intervention were dominated by the New Zealand and Australian governments, which negotiated most initial aspects of the arrangements with PNG (particularly those in relation to the TMG) and in general in close consultation with key Bougainvillean figures.[17]

Who Was Involved?

The involvement of representatives from both senior military and diplomatic branches in the joint New Zealand-Australia Resource Group that developed the detailed proposals for the TMG characterized not only the planning and the general implementation of the strategy of the intervention, but also the operation of the TMG and the PMG (for example, through the division of responsibilities between a military commander and a civilian chief negotiator).[18] Although the lead in planning was undertaken by the Australian and New Zealand departments for foreign affairs, the countries' defense departments and military organizations were deeply involved, and highly influential, in decisionmaking processes (sometimes to the chagrin of diplomats, who felt that military planners wanted more resources deployed than were necessary for the job). There was intense consultation between the Australian and New Zealand capital cities over arrangements for both the TMG and the PMG, especially in 1997 and 1998. Thereafter, the more intense and regular interaction was between the two countries' embassies to PNG on the one hand, and the PNG and Bougainville parties to the peace process on the other hand. There was also consultation with the governments of Fiji, Vanuatu, and Solomon Islands in relation to the roles that they were playing. The agreements between PNG and the four countries contributing to the TMG and PMG provided for a Peace Process Steering Committee as a mechanism for discussions between parties to the agreements. It met

17. For interesting perspectives on the part of a senior external adviser to the PNG government, see Wolfers, "International Peace Missions in Bougainville."

18. Roger Mortlock, first commander of the TMG, describes the success of the "Bougainville Intervention" as being the result of "intense cooperation between the military and diplomatic arms." See Mortlock, "Lessons from Bougainville," 471.

infrequently, mainly in the early years of the process, reviewing progress of the PMG and the peace process, and considering plans and prospects. The PPSC was at times a useful mechanism for consultation between the contributing countries, but was not otherwise an institution of central importance in the peace process.

Within the government systems in both New Zealand and Australia, interagency committees planned and oversaw the implementation of major steps. In the early stages, the senior civil servants with responsibility for the Bougainville peace process in both New Zealand and Australia were persons with long experience in the Pacific and PNG, and in relation to Bougainville in particular. They had played significant roles in some of the pre-1997 peace efforts, and in doing so had built relationships with key persons on all sides. This background was essential to the very effective manner in which they operated. The senior Australian civilian officers in the TMG and PMG also tended to have extensive PNG and Pacific experience, an important attribute in the situation where the military commanders usually had little.

The arrangements for involvement of the UN mission were negotiated between the PNG government and the UN Secretariat in New York, with careful consultation with the Bougainville parties.[19] As already discussed, there were at times tensions between the director of the UN mission and senior officials of the PMG. In general, however, they worked cooperatively, each supporting the other in a variety of ways.

The Importance of Just Being There

Some of those serving the PMG sometimes expressed a sense of frustration that they were not achieving enough or not making progress fast enough. Some talked openly about their wish to play a far more activist role, for example, by engaging directly with the parties, encouraging them to explore ways of resolving their differences, mediating disputes as they arose, and even undertaking significant development activities. In part, this attitude reflected the fact that PMG personnel served for quite brief periods during which it could often be difficult to see progress. It also reflected some frustration with a limited monitor-

19. For discussion of some of the issues involved from the PNG perspective, see Edward P. Wolfers, "International Peace Missions in Bougainville."

ing role, which did not always sit easily with the goal-oriented approaches of the military and key civil service bodies that senior PMG personnel and monitoring team members came from. But, in general, the senior leadership of the PMG understood that the most important service provided by the international community was a secure environment within which the initially extremely distrustful parties could build the trust and communication needed to negotiate outcomes that would make long-term peacebuilding a real possibility. To a large extent, that goal could be achieved merely by PMG's presence in Bougainville. (David Hallett, a senior Australian official who was the last chief negotiator in the PMG, notes that a Bougainvillean child, asked to describe the work of the PMG, said it was "to wave to people"—a reference to the efforts made by PMG monitoring teams to present a friendly face as they drove through villages and hamlets on their regular patrols mainly directed at ensuring awareness of the PMG's presence.) Beyond just being there, the PMG's other main contribution was to facilitate the involvement of locally based leaders from almost all main Bougainville factions. This was critically important for building support for the process and its outcomes where parties, as already discussed, were, in fact, loose coalitions.

Some Unintended Consequences of Donor Funding Arrangements

While donor funding was meant to facilitate or otherwise support peace process activities and was always supplied with the best of intentions, with regard to humanitarian and development assistance, it brought some unintended negative impacts. Four main kinds of funding require particular mention, all of which have contributed to a tendency for some Bougainvilleans to regard peace process activities as economic activities to some extent.

The first concerns projects, funded mainly early in the process, which were often classified as being "peace dividends"—mainly small-scale projects awarded to those communities supporting the peace process, such as building classrooms and health centers and assisting with small commercial projects. The term "peace dividends" was an unfortunate one under the circumstances, suggesting that peace was not necessarily something to be supported because of its inherent value but rather because of economic returns of some kind. Second, the UN mission, the UNDP, Australia, and New Zealand all offered allowances and other financial benefits to Bougainvilleans (and, in some cases, PNG government officials) attending peace process meetings and taking part in awareness activities. The funds were offered in good faith, mainly because most Bougainvilleans had little income at that time. But eventually, many people would not take part in peace process–related activities without some form of recompense.

Third, the UN mission and some donors made various forms of payment to facilitate customary reconciliation ceremonies. While they all ruled out any funding for the items usually exchanged as compensation (shell valuables and pigs), they did fund costs of facilitators, transport, and food. Fourth, in early 2001, when progress toward agreement on a weapons disposal process was poor, Australia offered financial incentives to groups of former combatants in communities disposing of weapons by providing monies from a fund of AUS$5 million for small commercial or other projects—another form of "dividends." Intense competition resulted, and the funds were perceived as having been unevenly distributed. Such incentives also reinforced the impression that participation in peace process activities was dependent on funding.

All of these well-intentioned initiatives added to overall perceptions that there was an almost unlimited pot of international funds available to support peace process–related activities. In a postconflict situation in which the people had long had limited access to income, the flow of funds from the international community undermined long-established patterns of self-reliance and contributed to unsustainable expectations, something that the ABG has had to deal with since its first election in 2005. Further, these funds negatively impacted the peace process by tending to offer economic advantages to Bougainvilleans with the closest international community connections, thereby adding to economic inequality (always a source of tensions and conflict in Bougainville) and opening some leaders to considerable public criticism.

Integrating the Intervention and the Locally Managed Aspects of the Peace Process

In general, the diverse aspects of the intervention were developed at the request of the parties. Requests initiating various aspects of the intervention, or giving extended mandates to, say, the PMG or the UN mission, were generally made by the parties through the negotiation process, often recorded as part of agreements such as the Burnham Truce, the Lincoln Agreement, or the April 1998 ceasefire. Others involved direct requests of one party or another, as with requests for technical support to the various teams involved in negotiating the political agreement.

Formal consultative and decisionmaking mechanisms established as part of the process handled, or contributed to managing, the relationship of various aspects of the international intervention to the peace process. These included the PPCC, in which both the PMG and the UN mission participated, and the PPSC. There were also informal mechanisms, including regular meetings held among the TMG or PMG, the UN mission, and Bougainville parties. TMG and PMG commanders and the director of the UN mission made regular visits to Port Moresby, where they briefed senior political leaders and officials on developments in Bougainville. In the process, misunderstandings were often resolved and communications maintained.

5

The 2001 Political Settlement and Its Implementation through 2010

Heavily dependent on indirect international intervention, the negotiation and implementation of the Bougainville Peace Agreement signed on August 30, 2001, were critically important aspects of the peacebuilding process. Negotiation of the agreement faced many difficulties in a situation where the divisions were not only multidimensional but also changing. Yet all parties to the process—as well as the international facilitators—were clear that achieving agreement between the main Bougainvillean factions first, and then between Bougainville and PNG, was of critical importance to achieving a degree of reconciliation both between opposing Bougainvillean groups and between Bougainville and PNG. The agreement itself is unusual when compared with peace agreements elsewhere, both in terms of content and of the extent to which the parties have cooperated in ensuring its implementation.

The contributions of the international intervention to the negotiating of the peace agreement, outlined in the previous chapter, were for the most part indirect, with the parties generally managing the negotiation process themselves. Contributions of a different kind have continued in relation to the critically important phase of the peace process since August 2001, during which the peace agreement has been implemented.

Political Negotiations across Two Deep Divides

The two major distinct dimensions of the Bougainville conflict (involving, first, PNG versus BRA/BIG and, second, the opposing Bougainville factions) meant that, to some extent, two similarly distinct processes were required to conclude a political settlement.[1] The first process

1. For more detail on the issues surrounding the Bougainville Peace Agreement touched on in this section, see Regan, "The Bougainville Political Settlement"; Spark and Bailey, "Disarmament in Bougainville"; Yash Ghai and Anthony J. Regan, with Y. P.

involved developing a common negotiating position among the deeply divided Bougainvillean factions (some in strong support of integration into PNG and others committed to early secession). The second involved the combined Bougainville parties reaching a compromise with a PNG government that was deeply opposed to even a deferred referendum on secession and to some degree fearful of the potentially divisive impacts for the rest of PNG of even special Bougainville autonomy arrangements. These processes have been discussed elsewhere and so are just highlighted here.[2]

It was in June 1999 that a common negotiating position was developed by the BPC (a position later accepted by the dissident pro-integration leaders, as discussed above).[3] As the BPC included key leaders from most of the main opposing factions, it had to take account of positions strongly supportive of early secession through to strong support for integration. When it first met after being elected, bridging those differences appeared to present insurmountable problems. The first step involved advisers to all factions jointly developing nine options for future political arrangements for Bougainville—ranging from immediate independence to full integration into PNG. Next the advisers assigned tentative ratings to each option—high, medium, or low—based on assessments of how well the option in question could contribute to dealing with the needs of postconflict Bougainville as reflected against 20 criteria. These criteria took account of such key issues as Bougainville's long-term secessionist movement, grievances that had contributed to the

---

Ghai, "Unitary State, Devolution, Autonomy, Secession: State Building and Nation Building in Bougainville, Papua New Guinea," in *The Round Table*, vol. 95, no. 386 (2006): 589–608; Edward P. Wolfers, "Bougainville Autonomy—Implications for Governance and Decentralisation," Public Policy in Papua New Guinea—Discussion Paper Series, 2006/5 (Canberra: State, Society and Governance in Melanesia Program, Australian National University, 2006); Anthony J. Regan, "Resolving the Bougainville Self-Determination Dispute: Autonomy or Complex Power-Sharing?" in *Self-Determination Disputes: Complex Power-Sharing in Theory and Practice* (Leiden: Martinus Nijhoff Publishers, 2008), 125–60.

2. See Carl and Garasu, eds., *Weaving Consensus*, and Boege and Garasu, "Papua New Guinea."

3. See Anthony J. Regan, "Resolving Two Dimensions of Conflict—The Dynamics of Consent, Consensus and Compromise," in Carl and Garasu, eds., *Weaving Consensus*, 36–42.

conflict, PNG opposition to secession, Bougainville's weak economic base and low level of administrative capacity, and so on. This process resulted in the highest rating being clearly given to one particular option. It involved a constitutionally guaranteed but deferred referendum on independence for Bougainville from PNG combined with a high level of autonomy for Bougainville during the period of deferral.

Next, the advisers' analysis was discussed at length by the BPC, which eventually agreed with the assessment of the advisers that the highest rating option provided the best basis for a compromise solution. This option balanced the interests of opposing factions by keeping the question of secession alive, but would leave an ultimate decision on the choice between secession and integration to a later democratic process for all Bougainvilleans conducted when disarmament had been completed, reconciliation achieved, and the economy restored. After the BPC had reached agreement in this way, the common Bougainville negotiating position was further developed by expanding the details of the chosen option. Initially this common negotiating position called for a five- to six-year deferral of the referendum, which would have an outcome binding on the parties.[4] In other words, if a majority of Bougainvilleans were to vote "yes" to independence, then PNG would be constitutionally obliged to accept and implement that decision.

Bougainville's common negotiating position was first put to PNG in talks on June 30, 1999, and from that point set the agenda for the negotiations. One difficulty arising from the way the negotiating position was developed was that the Bougainville negotiating team found difficulties in making compromises; its position was already the product of difficult factional compromises. For its part, PNG opposed the referendum proposal as undermining national sovereignty. The autonomy demanded was seen as not only too close to independence, and thus inimical to PNG sovereignty, but also divisive and likely to undermine the viability of the central state. PNG's negotiators sought to moderate the autonomy proposals through suggestions for cooperative arrangements that might

4. The processes followed to identify and assess the options for future political arrangements and to agree on Bougainville's common negotiating position are described in more detail in Regan, "Resolving Two Dimensions of Conflict."

encourage a reasonable degree of integration of Bougainville into national arrangements.

Ultimately, compromises were reached. They were achieved through a long and tortuous negotiation process, competent chairing, and some mediation on difficult issues. Of the more than 20 negotiation sessions, some lasted as long as three weeks. The chairing was, for the most part, left in the hands of the director of the UN mission, Noel Sinclair, who managed the often tense process with patience and good humor. Examples of mediation by the UN mission and Australia on two of the most significant ones, both in relation to the highly contentious referendum issue, are covered next.

Overview of Key Aspects of the 2001 Bougainville Peace Agreement

The agreement contains innovative solutions to difficult issues that initially divided the distrustful parties.[5] The three main elements involve arrangements for a referendum on Bougainville's independence, demilitarization, and a high level of autonomy for Bougainville, with a large part of the arrangements to be provided for by amendment to the PNG National Constitution. Two other important and creative elements of the agreement include an unusual degree of constitutional protection for the agreed arrangements and the provision of incentives to implement the agreement.

Referendum on Independence

The most unusual of the agreement's three main elements involves a provision for the holding of a constitutionally guaranteed referendum for Bougainvilleans on Bougainville's independence. Mediation by the UN mission was required in March 2000 just to get PNG to agree to include the referendum issue on the negotiating agenda. In December 2000 mediation by Alexander Downer, then the Australian minister for foreign affairs and trade, achieved a compromise that ended what had by November 2000 seemed to be an intractable deadlock on the issue,

5. The full text of the agreement can be viewed at www.c-r.org/our-work/accord/png-bougainville/key-texts37.php (accessed August 10, 2009) or at www.usip.org/library/pa/bougainville/bougain_20010830.html (accessed June 1, 2007).

one which had threatened the negotiations and the peace process itself. Downer was acting on the advice of the Australian ambassador to PNG, Nick Warner, and one of his senior officers (Sarah Storey) who had been a peace monitor in the TMG before being posted by the Australian Department of Foreign Affairs and Trade to the Australian embassy position responsible for monitoring developments in Bougainville. Both Warner and Storey had developed a close interest and good understanding of the Bougainville situation, and Downer trusted their judgment and advice. Downer achieved the compromise in separate informal talks, one with the key leaders of the main Bougainville factions in December 2000, and subsequent discussions with the PNG prime minister (Mekere Morauta) and a few key ministers. The talks were held in the absence of advisers, largely because they were informal discussions that had not been expected to deal with such critically important issues, and so it had not been thought necessary for advisers to be present. On the Bougainville side, in particular, the absence of advisers may have been of critical importance, as at least some of the advisers would probably have argued strongly that the compromise Downer proposed offered too little protection to concerns of the pro-secession parts of the Bougainville negotiators about achieving a clear path to independence.

Under the compromise, a referendum would in fact be held, but it would be deferred for a minimum of 10 and a maximum of 15 years after the establishment of an autonomous Bougainville government (rather than Bougainville's initially preferred five to six years). Most significant was the concession from the Bougainville side that the referendum outcome would not be binding, but, rather, subject to ultimate authority of the PNG parliament, following consultation among the parties. This compromise salved PNG's concerns on safeguarding sovereignty, while Bougainville was persuaded to agree to a nonbinding outcome in part by Downer's suggestion that an extended period of deferral would offer a more realistic period within which the differences among Bougainvilleans on the issue of independence could be resolved, and more especially by his assurance that PNG could hardly ignore an overwhelming vote in favor of independence. In the course of the discussions, the Bougainville leaders are clear that Downer implied that the international community would encourage PNG to honor such a vote, and he referred to East Timor's experience as a precedent in this regard. (The referendum on autonomy for East Timor held in 1999 was not legally binding on the Indonesian government. Downer's point being that an overwhelming vote in favor of independence was not ignored by the international community, which applied pressure on Indonesia to honor the outcome.) It was implied that because the international community had been so committed to the Bougainville peace process, that community would want its "investment" in the process protected, and so would continue to be involved in Bougainville in the lead-up to the referendum, ensuring that there would be pressure on PNG to honor the referendum outcome.

On the PNG side, however, the implications of Downer's assurances in relation to recognition of sovereignty were that PNG would have the right to ignore the outcome of the referendum if it wished, and that the international community would understand its position if it did so.

The key difficulty inherent in the compromise is that both PNG and the Bougainville parties now tend to see the international community, and Australia in particular, as the ultimate guarantor of what could readily be diametrically opposed positions following the referendum. In a sense, there is a risk that there has merely been a deferral of the point in time when confrontation on the issue of independence occurs.

Autonomy

The most complex of the agreement's three main elements involves arrangements for a high level of autonomy for Bougainville in the period up to when the referendum is held—and beyond that if Bougainville remains part of PNG after the referendum. Under the agreement (as implemented in the PNG constitution), Bougainville is empowered to use consultative processes to develop its own subnational constitution to determine the name, structures, and processes of an autonomous government for Bougainville. That government (named the Autonomous Bougainville Government in the Bougainville constitution adopted in 2004) has available to it full legislative powers on most subjects of concern to modern governments. These include subjects of the greatest sensitivity in relation to the origins of the conflict—such as land, minerals, petroleum, ocean resources, and the environment. The ABG can also establish its own separate police force, bureaucracy, courts, and ombudsmen, and can impose a wide range of taxes. Significantly, it even has some powers over limited aspects of foreign affairs and defense.

The postconflict situation, however, left the capacity of the ABG administrative arm largely destroyed and meant that the ABG would initially have neither the trained officials nor the funding resources needed to exercise its potential powers and functions. Further, existing PNG laws already covered most of the new subject areas made available to the ABG. As a result, rather than immediately invest the ABG with all its potential powers, the agreement initially only makes these powers available for transfer from the national government. The ABG can initiate transfer of any particular function or power by giving 12 months notice of its intention to assume the function or power and then working with the PNG government to make joint plans to develop the capacity necessary to exercise the function or power in question.

Demilitarization of Bougainville—PNG Forces Withdraw and Bougainvilleans Disarm

The third main element of the agreement—demilitarization of Bougainville—is a goal pursued by providing for withdrawal of PNG security forces and limiting their future deployment, establishing a three-stage process for disarmament of the BRA and the BRF (a process referred to in the agreement as "disposal of weapons"), offering amnesty and pardon for any former combatants who may have committed conflict-related criminal offenses, and disbanding the Bougainvillean combatant organizations, namely the BRA, the BRF, and (it was hoped) the MDF. The stages to the agreed-upon weapons disposal process included, first, collecting weapons into containers secured with keys held by ex-combatant unit commanders; second, consolidating the contained weapons into more centrally located double-locked containers, with second keys held by the UN observer mission; third, ultimately disposing of the weapons, with the method of disposal to be agreed to by the parties within four and a half months after the UN mission had verified that the second stage of disposal had been successfully completed.

Protecting Agreed Arrangements from Unilateral Change

Constitutional protection for the resulting peace arrangements is provided through their inclusion in the PNG National Constitution and an Organic Law authorized by the amendments to the constitution (the Organic Law on Peace-Building in Bougainville—perhaps the only constitutional law in the world incorporating the term peacebuilding). Both sets of constitutional provisions (the amendments to the National Constitution and the Organic Law) were made subject to special procedural requirements that must be met by all proposed laws amending the PNG National Constitution (special parliamentary majorities, two separate votes held at least two months apart, and so on). The Bougainvilleans also insisted on, and PNG ultimately conceded, a further and more onerous level of constitutional protection—consent of the Bougainville legislature for any proposed amendment to a constitutional provision in relation to Bougainville (arrangements referred to by the Bougainville leaders as "double entrenchment").

There were two significant reasons why the Bougainvillean parties saw constitutionalization of the arrangements as offering considerable protection from unilateral alteration of the agreed arrangements by PNG. First, PNG had a reasonably good record of respect for its National Constitution, with constitutional rulings by the Supreme Court against the national government being respected by the government. Second, it was assumed that the international community would maintain a "watching brief" on PNG adherence to the arrangements.

Embedding Implementation Incentives

The agreement embeds incentives for its implementation through creative arrangements on the sequencing of, and linkages between, agreed-upon steps for implementation of key arrangements.[6] The main linkages are among the provisions, on the one hand, for disposal of weapons by Bougainvillean factions and, on the other hand, the withdrawal of PNG forces from Bougainville, and, more important, the

6. For further discussion of incentives and conditions built into the agreement, see Anthony J. Regan, "External Versus Internal Incentives in Peace Processes: The Bougainville Experience," in *Accord*, no. 19; *Powers of Persuasion: Incentives, Sanctions and Conditionality in Peacemaking* (London: Conciliation Resources, 2008), 44–49.

constitutionalizing and implementation of the agreed arrangements. The linkages involved completion of steps agreed to by one party being specified as a "condition precedent" to be completed before the other party is required to take a separate step.

In particular, the obligation that Bougainville's ex-combatant groups move weapons to secure storage arose only when PNG both passed the constitutional amendments implementing the agreement and began withdrawal of its forces from Bougainville. However, in order to maintain pressure on Bougainville groups to dispose of their weapons, after the constitutional amendments implementing the agreement were passed by parliament, they did not come into operation until the UN mission verified completion of stage 2 of weapons disposal (secure containment). In this way, the PNG government honored its commitment to constitutionalize the peace agreement, while at the same time pressure was applied to the Bougainville combatants to dispose of their weapons, for they did not get the benefit of the new constitutional laws actually operating until a previously agreed degree of progress in weapons disposal was independently verified. In short, progress in weapons disposal was critical in determining when the autonomy arrangements began to operate, and the point at when the "clock" for determining the date of holding the referendum began "ticking." Lack of substantial compliance with the agreed-upon weapons disposal process could also result in the UN mission delaying elections for the ABG (any party to the agreement could call on the UN to verify and certify substantial compliance in weapons disposal and whether the level of security for the weapons was conducive to the holding of elections). All factions were thereby given incentives to honor obligations with which they might otherwise have been reluctant to comply. An additional linkage yet to come into operation is intended to provide ongoing incentives for continued efforts in relation to weapons disposal. It involves setting the date for holding the referendum within a period of 10 to 15 years after the ABG is established. Among the conditions to be taken into account when setting that date is the progress made in disposing of weapons.

Implementation of the Agreement to Early 2010

The implementation process to date can conveniently be broken into two main periods. One involves the four years from the signing of the peace agreement to establishing the ABG in June 2005. The second is the first five years of operation of the ABG.

The parties were well aware that implementation of the political settlements intended to resolve the conflict was paramount, and that failure to do so could lead to a renewal of the conflict. Concern about implementation of the agreement figured prominently, first while those involved drafted the constitutional laws giving effect to the agreement (see discussion under "Constitutionalization of the Agreement") and second through their participation in the Joint Supervisory Body, a mechanism provided for in the agreement, representing both sides of the conflict and established specifically to oversee implementation. It is perhaps one of the clearest measures of the broad success of the Bougainville peace process that implementation has generally proceeded well—if sometimes more slowly than anticipated—and that it has clearly contributed to resolution of the original conflict (notwithstanding the localized conflict in south Bougainville that occurred from late 2005 to 2009, as discussed in chapter 6).

Constitutionalization of the Agreement

The amendments to the PNG National Constitution (together with the associated Organic Law) needed to give effect to the agreement were drafted under the guidance of a joint committee of PNG government and Bougainville advisers and completed by November 2001. The amendments and the Organic Law were both approved by the PNG parliament by separate votes in January and March 2002. Both the PNG government and the autonomous government established for Bougainville in 2005 (below) have in general been at pains to adhere to the requirements of the constitution and the Organic Law. To date there has yet to be a dispute that has required judicial interpretation of the constitutional arrangements.

Demilitarization of Bougainville, 2001–05

Withdrawal of the PNG security forces from Bougainville began late in 2001 and was completed by 2003. Implementation of the agreed weapons disposal process (placing of BRA and BRF weapons into single-locked containers) also began late in 2001, and in August 2003 the UN mission verified that the second stage of weapons disposal (more secure containerization, with double locks) had occurred, thereby bringing into operation the constitutional amendments implementing the agreement. The means to dispose of the contained weapons was agreed upon by the parties in December 2003, and by May 2005, 95 percent (more than 1,900) of the weapons that had been contained had been destroyed, and the UN mission announced completion of stage 3 of the disposal process. The first decision of the PNG National Court under the amnesty provisions was handed down in April 2005 (amnesty being accorded to a former BRA member charged with murder committed during the conflict).

It is unknown what proportion of total weapons was represented by the 1,900 plus weapons destroyed by May 2005, but this number was certainly only a part of the total held by the Bougainvillean former combatant groups. In verifying the second stage of containment, the UN mission director in his July 2003 report acknowledged as much.[7] Caches of undisposed weapons were a significant factor in the violent localized conflict that occurred in south Bougainville from late 2005 to 2008. A brief explanation is required both as to the extent of these weapons and why the UN mission verified completion of the second stage of containment despite being aware of such weapons.

Several categories of weapons had not been contained by July 2003. In particular, Ona's MDF did not participate in the UNOMB-supervised weapons disposal. It was estimated by senior BRA figures at the time that the MDF held about 400 to 500 weapons. Though more recent estimates by former BRA and MDF leaders who, since 2009, have been seeking to facilitate development of a weapons disposal process involving

7. Noel Sinclair, "Report by the Director of UNOMB Verifying and Certifying the Achievement of Stage Two of the Weapons Disposal Plan Contained in the Bougainville Peace Agreement," unpublished report of the United Nations Observer Mission Bougainville, July 2003.

the MDF elements in the former "no-go-zone" in the vicinity of the Panguna mine (see Map 6), suggest that there could be a much greater number of weapons in the hands of MDF elements—perhaps as many as 2,500 (including a substantial, though as yet unknown, number of WWII weapons as well as significant amounts of ammunition from the former U.S.-Australian World War II base at Torokina, most obtained since 2005). It was also generally understood in 2003 (and subsequently) that BRA and BRF elements in various areas retained some weapons, in part in order to counterbalance the failure of the MDF to participate in the process and in part because of lingering uncertainty about what action PNG forces might take. For example, if PNG were to refuse to honor a Bougainville referendum vote in favor of independence. There were still other BRA and BRF groups—mainly in south Bougainville—that also retained weapons to improve their own security because of lack of reconciliation of localized conflicts that had occurred during the period of the main Bougainville conflict. Some criminal elements also had retained weapons obtained when they had been members of BRA and BRA elements, or they had been able to acquire weapons from former combatants.

As to why the UN mission verified completion of the second stage of weapon disposal—first, the verification decision was made only after extensive community consultation across Bougainville in which there was strong support for verification to occur. At the time, the situation in Bougainville generally, including the south, seemed peaceful, and the risk of resumption of even localized violent conflict seemed remote. In addition, the UN mission director judged that by delaying verification, the effective dates for implementing the peace agreement and progress toward setting up the ABG also would be delayed. Such a setback would likely lead to frustration due to failure to meet high expectations and perhaps contribute to popular support for Ona (who remained highly critical of the peace process). In addition, the UN director's report noted that it was widely accepted that once the ABG was established, the new government would itself be able to advance the process to dispose of remaining weapons. This could be achieved by working toward reconciliation with the groups outside the peace process, by developing a Bougainville police service, and so on. A further safeguard offered was the possibility of applying pressure at a later stage if it was found that after verification of the completion of stage two, weapons were still not secure. In particular, under the Bougainville Peace Agreement the UN mission had the power to delay elections for the autonomous government if it were to certify that the weapons subject to the weapons disposal process were not secure.

In the end, the assessment by the UN mission director was accepted by not only the leaders of the Bougainville parties but also the PNG government. As it happened, there was no significant problem with weapons in the lead-up to the ABG elections (other than the refusal of one major BRA group in south Bougainville to destroy weapons it had contained), so the possibility of delaying the ABG elections as a means of applying pressure to improve the level of weapons disposal was never seriously considered.

To complicate matters, as noted above, there were also other sources of weapons in Bougainville in addition to those considered in the UN mission director's July 2003 report. First, that report assumed that all securely contained weapons would ultimately be disposed of in accordance with the agreed plan. In fact, some of those contained weapons were not destroyed. In particular, the BRA group in the south of Bougainville (the Buin area) that refused to destroy its weapoms held more than 40 high-powered modern weapons that had been contained. When new rounds of localized conflict broke out in south Bougainville in 2006 with a former BRA group that had from 2003 developed links with the MDF, those weapons were removed from their container and utilized (see the discussion of the Bougainville Freedom Fighters in chapter 6).

Also during this postconflict period, significant concerns arose about access to the weapons and ammunition that had been dumped in Bougainville during World War II. Between 2006 and 2010 some residents living in and around the former U.S. and Australian base at Torokina, one of the least developed areas of Bougainville, have made great efforts to locate such material. Reliable reports indicate that since 2006 several hundred World War II weapons (including many submachine guns) and large quantities of ammunition have been dug up or retrieved from rivers, drains, and lakes, and sold or otherwise supplied to armed groups, particularly in south Bougainville, as well as to criminals and other individuals both in Bougainville and in other parts of PNG. During the same period, increased effectiveness of restrictions on importation into PNG of weapons from Australia and elsewhere has resulted in dramatic increases in prices paid (both in Bougainville and elsewhere in PNG) for working World War II weapons and ammunition, providing a considerable incentive for people to locate such material. Largely as a result of such market pressures, it seems that many more working weapons and ammunition have been found since 2006 than during the whole of the main Bougainville conflict (1988–97).

With the departure of the UN mission from Bougainville in mid-2005, the main pressure on groups and individuals to dispose of weapons neither contained nor destroyed was removed. More generally, there is evidence of some trade in weapons, between individuals and groups in Bougainville, and from Bougainville to other parts of PNG. From 2008 the continuing availability of weapons and their use in localized conflict in Bougainville have resulted in moves to develop a new weapons disposal process, as touched on in brief in chapter 6.

In terms of disbanding of the Bougainvillean former combatant organizations, the peace agreement provided that "the former combatant groups should be disbanded as soon as they no longer have a role in relation to the implementation of the weapons disposal plan provided for under [the] Agreement."[8] Of course, by the time the UNOMB supervised process was completed in June 2005, only the BRA and the BRF were participating in the process, so the requirement for disbanding could only be applied to them and not to the MDF. But the former organizations accepted the requirement for disbanding. At the same time, however, provisions were included in the Bougainville constitution that created three seats in the legislature for the Autonomous Bougainville Government to be reserved for former combatants. The PNG government expressed some concern when the Bougainville constitution was being prepared that elected representation for former combatants could offend the requirements of the peace agreement on disbanding their organizations. Such concerns were dealt with by establishing a unified body for all former combatants and vesting it with responsibility

8. Bougainville Peace Agreement, paragraph 344(b).

for determining (for the purposes of qualifications to stand for election to a seat for former combatants) which persons are, in fact, former combatants. In this way, the BRA and the BRF were regarded as disbanding and their members jointly forming a single organization that now had peaceful political purposes.

Establishing and Operating the Autonomous Bougainville Government

As discussed already, the implementation incentives in the Bougainville Peace Agreement delayed drawing up a constitution until the second stage of weapons disposal had been certified as complete. As a result, Bougainville leaders were unable to draw up a constitution for the ABG between 2001 and early 2002—the period immediately after the PNG parliament had passed the amendments to the PNG National Constitution (as well as the Organic Law) intended to implement the peace agreement. By late 2002, however, it was clear that UN verification was very likely to occur by mid-2003, and so with PNG government agreement, a consultative constitution-making process provided for under the Bougainville Peace Agreement began in September 2002. In the next 26 months, until November 2004, a broadly representative 24-member Bougainville Constitutional Commission (BCC), including three women representatives nominated by the Bougainville Provincial Council of Women, consulted widely throughout Bougainville and with parts of the Bougainville diaspora living elsewhere in PNG. Close consultation with the PNG government was also required, because it had ultimate authority to withhold ratification of the Bougainville constitution if it had sufficient grounds to believe that the proposed document was not consistent with the peace agreement. In September 2004 the BCC's final draft constitution, together with a detailed report explaining the draft, was presented to a broadly representative Bougainville Constituent Assembly (comprised of the members of both the BPC and the BIPG). In November 2004 the assembly adopted a slightly amended version of the draft. PNG government endorsement of the new Bougainville constitution occurred in December 2004.

The innovative constitution provided for holding ABG elections using a "first-past-the-post" (simple plurality) voting system.[9] The first general elections, held in May 2005, were for a directly elected president who sits in the legislature and heads a cabinet of ministers selected from among the 39 members elected to represent constituencies. The constitution provides for 33 single-member constituencies and three regional constituencies where all enrolled voters can cast votes for two members—one of whom must be a woman and one a former combatant. To put it another way, three seats are reserved for women and three for former combatants, although all voters (not just women and former combatants) vote for the representatives for these special seats. The legislature is chaired by a speaker who cannot be a member of the legislature, and is selected by vote of the members of the legislature.

As of early 2010, the ABG had been operating for almost five years. The Bougainville constitution and the political institutions initially established under it have operated reasonably well. The legislature has passed numerous mainly machinery and procedural laws, including some significant ones, such as the long detailed Bougainville Elections Act 2007. Several new institutions necessary for the operation of the ABG have been established, notably a Bougainville Electoral Commission, which has conducted a Bougainville-wide by-election for the office of president, made necessary by the death of the first president in mid-2008. So far the legislature has not passed any significant laws on the wide range of legislative functions and powers made available to the ABG under the amendments to the PNG constitution implementing the peace agreement, mainly because the process for the transfer of control from the PNG government over such matters has been much slower than expected, as discussed below.

For the most part, the funding provided to the ABG by the PNG government has been in accordance with the minimum requirements of the financial provisions of the constitutional laws implementing the Bougainville Peace Agreement, though undoubtedly less than had been

9. The constitution requires that in subsequent elections the same limited preferential voting system introduced in PNG national elections after the 2002 general elections should also be used in Bougainville, so that system was used in the by-election for president held in December 2008.

hoped for by some Bougainville leaders, who had envisaged that the PNG would use more generous funding than the peace agreement and the law required as a means of encouraging Bougainvilleans to consider integration into PNG rather than secession (in the referendum on independence). That such hopes have not been met has probably been a factor in what seems to be growing support amongst Bougainvilleans for a vote in favor of independence. Such sentiment received a considerable boost late in 2009.

In late 2009, when the 2010 budget was approved by the parliament, no provision was included for the restoration and development grant payable to the ABG annually under the Constitutional laws implementing the peace agreement; the grant had been expected to be PNGK15 million (about US$5 million) for 2010. This omission was a complete surprise to the ABG, and the reasons for its omission remain obscure. At a meeting of the Joint Supervisory Body in December 2009, the PNG deputy prime minister indicated that there had been a misunderstanding, in part related to other kinds of funding allocated to the ABG, which PNG authorities regarded as more than compensating for failure to pay the grant. However, the deputy prime minister appeared to accept that the grant should have been paid and indicated that he and relevant PNG authorities would work to ensure that it was. Early in 2010 an initial allocation of PNGK5 million of the PNGK15 million was made available, with statements made that it was hoped that the balance of PNGK10 million would also be found. This episode has caused considerable tension and contributed to some concern among some Bougainville leaders who question whether the PNG government is truly committed to implementation of the peace agreement. While most leaders do not yet have such doubts, the episode does underline the ease with which the national government could lose support in Bougainville should it be perceived as losing interest in implementing the peace agreement.

In relation to the bureaucracy, the ABG has authority to direct and control its administrative arm—the Bougainville administration—which comprises several hundred officers of the PNG public service. They provide a range of services and carry out numerous duties, all related to the functions and powers of the previous provincial government, including education, health, and similar basic services. These are the foundation functions and powers of the ABG. Considerable efforts have been made to improve the capacity of the administration, in particular through a significant restructure and recruitment exercise, and through capacity-building support requested from AusAID and New Zealand AID (see below). One significant obstacle has been the difficulty in attracting former experienced Bougainvilleans living outside Bougainville to return to jobs in postconflict Bougainville, where services and the general conditions of life are much reduced when compared to many major urban centers elsewhere in PNG.

Transfer of Functions and Powers to the ABG

The first of the major new powers and functions available to Bougainville—control of police—was delegated by the national government to the provincial government in December 2003 and inherited by the ABG when the new government was established. However, the full extent of Bougainville's police power was never made entirely clear by the terms of the delegating instrument, a matter that causes the ABG ongoing concern.

The ABG has made several formal requests to the PNG government for transfer of further functions and powers. The main ones have been a request in November 2006 that powers relating to mining, oil, and gas regulation be transferred, and in February 2009 a request that some basic functions, such as setting time zones, establishing women's organizations, and licensing the sale of alcoholic beverages, in addition to others related to the functions and powers inherited by the ABG from the previous provincial government.

The requirement (under the peace agreement) for the two governments to jointly develop plans to provide such new capacity and resources as the ABG may need for effective exercise of new functions and powers can sometimes be met readily. The most clear case is where there are already PNG government officials based in Bougainville and exercising functions under the auspices of PNG government public sector agencies. In such cases, capacity can be provided by simply transferring control of the staff to the ABG at the same time as control over the function in question. But many of the functions and powers made available to the ABG have never been exercised by government officials based in Bougainville, and so before a transfer can be agreed, it is necessary to create and fund public service positions; locate funding for housing, offices, equipment, and operations; and recruit the staff, train them, and so on. These considerations apply in relation to the November 2006 ABG request for transfer of the complex set of mining, oil, and gas functions and powers. Largely because there was no precedent, it took more than 12 months to agree to the necessary arrangements for gradual transfer of the functions and powers, and the implementation of those arrangements has itself moved slowly, giving rise to some frustration on the part of the ABG. However, initial steps were taken in 2008, and by early 2010 arrangements were under way to fund and recruit the new staff needed to exercise the first major functions in relation to mining (involving the grant of mineral exploration licenses). Further, in March 2010 formal transfer of the basic functions and powers requested in February 2009 was announced by the national government. Hence, halting progress is being made on implementation of transfer arrangements. The progress is much slower than had been expected when the ABG was established, causing some frustration among Bougainville leaders. These delays may also tend to add to increased support for independence.

Relations between Governments

In general, relations between the ABG and the PNG government have been quite positive. The first stage of implementation (from 2001 to 2005) took much longer than expected, resulting in both some frustration in Bougainville and concern that PNG's possible agenda was to delay establishing the ABG for as long as possible, perhaps with a view to delaying the holding of the referendum (as under the peace agreement the referendum must be held no earlier than 10 and no later than 15 years after the autonomous government is established). However, the agreement was complex, and much of what was required to implement it was unprecedented and not always easy to achieve. Ultimately, despite the slow pace at which anticipated steps sometimes unfolded, everything agreed to was actually done, and in the process relations between the

PNG government and even the most critical Bougainvillean leaders participating in the process were much improved.

In the second stage—establishing and operating the ABG—much more of the responsibility for implementation falls directly on the ABG political institutions and the Bougainville administration. At the same time, much is still expected of the PNG government in terms of providing funds, cooperating in the transfer of functions and powers, and so on. Again, tension has sometimes been evident, especially relating to issues about the slow progress in transfer of functions and powers. However, the complexity of the steps required is certainly a contributing factor, as has been fast turnover in senior public servants at the national level with responsibility for implementing the arrangements. The Joint Supervisory Body, intended to oversee the implementation process, has met at least twice each year (as required by the peace agreement and the implementing laws) and has performed a useful role as a forum to deal with difficulties and find ways to resolve issues such as those relating to the transfer of functions and powers and the initial failure of the PNG government to allocate funds for the ABG's Restoration and Development Grant in the 2010 national budget.

International Community Roles after the PMG and UN Departures

Despite the departure of the main elements of the international intervention (the PMG as of mid-2003 and the UN mission mid-2005), the international community has continued to play significant roles in the implementation of the Bougainville Peace Agreement. Donor countries are chiefly involved, notably Australia and New Zealand, but there are some other important contributors, as outlined below.

AusAID and New Zealand Aid continue to provide various assistance to the ABG, in many respects similar to those described earlier in this monograph. New Zealand supports a range of small development projects and also puts significant resources into police capacity building. The latter includes direct support to the regular police, as well as long-term support for rural-based and part-time auxiliary police (training, payment of allowances, and the like). AusAID provides significant support to the police and to the law and justice sector more generally. Four senior advisers work full time with the Bougainville police (working to improve financial management, procurement, programming, and prosecution functions), and there is an extensive infrastructure construction and refurbishment program (court houses, police stations, community justice centers, and police housing, for instance).

AusAID also continues to fund maintenance of the main coastal trunk road, the critically important backbone of the Bougainville transport system. Beginning in 2008, that work has extended to parts of the road system not previously covered by the project, inclusive of the main road through the "no-go-zone" in central Bougainville (as discussed below). Further, the road project is increasingly focused on building the technical capacity within the Bougainville administration needed so it can handle the road maintenance program on an ongoing basis in the long term.

AusAID has supported the Bougainville administration in other ways as well. First, since 2004 an innovative project has provided incentives for improving the administration's weak planning, budgeting, and accountability capacity. Under a special funding mechanism—the Governance and Implementation Fund (GIF)—about PNGK6 million per year (about US$2 million), which sits outside the ABG budget framework but is allocated to the ABG (with some also to the PNG government)—goes to projects and programs selected jointly by the ABG, AusAID, and PNG and is directed to implementing the agreed autonomy arrangements and encouraging good government. The GIF arrangements envisage gradually increased funding levels that should ultimately be transferred to full ABG control (through the ABG budget and finance systems), but only if ABG capacity for budgeting and financial management improves. Second, since 2005, several mainly part-time technical advisers (a legislative drafter, a constitutional adviser, and others) have been made available to the Bougainville administration, as required. Third, from early 2009, eight full-time advisers from a number of countries are working with different parts of the administration as requested by the head of the administration.

The small UNDP office in Bougainville has worked with the ABG in a number of ways, inclusive of some capacity-building work and in reviewing policies in critical areas. For example, the ABG reviewed the local-level government system, which is intended to incorporate traditional chiefs and clan leaders, if the people of any particular area choose to establish their government in that way; such a system can contribute to administrative difficulties in the absence of adequate monitoring, training and resourcing, which the Bougainville administration has difficulty in providing adequately. In response to concerns about the escalating localized armed conflict in south Bougainville since about 2007 (discussed in chapter 6), the UNDP has also provided some support to ABG peacebuilding efforts involving local reconciliation and development of a new weapons disposal program, and has brought in experts to help consider fresh options in disposing of weapons. These efforts have, for the most part, been funded by AusAID, which views the UNDP as having a "comparative advantage" in supporting efforts in weapons disposal and reconciliation, largely because many Bougainvilleans perceive the agency as part of the same UN that provided the UNOMB to Bougainville. In fact, the UNDP has tended to be slow and disorganized and sometimes adds to problems. In particular, it has raised expectations when proposing to find funds for major programs, then subsequently contributed to local tensions when those funds could not be located.

A new and unexpected source of international community support emerging in 2009–10 has been the U.S. State Department. It was early in 2009 that the ABG was so concerned about the increased attempts to dig up World War II weapons and ammunition at Torokina that the ABG president approached the United States government for assistance. In June that year a small team from the U.S. State Department's Office of Weapons Removal and Abatement visited Torokina to assess the extent of the problem. The mission of that office is not to conduct clean-up operations in areas where U.S. military forces have operated, but rather to ensure that bombs, land mines, and other ordnance are removed from post-conflict sites, such as Angola, Cambodia, or (former) Yugoslavia, where such materials can constitute a grave obstacle to peacebuilding and economic development. The team that visited in June 2009 was reported to be satisfied that the situation in Torokina was within its mandate. Subsequently a team from a contracting company undertook a more detailed inspection over about a week in September 2009, reporting back that it had mapped almost 150 sites where it had identified unexploded bombs, artillery and mortar rounds, large sea mines, land mines, light weapons, and ammunition, and assessed that the material was undermining peacebuilding efforts. Early in 2010 the ABG received advice from the Office of Weapons Removal and Abatement that approval had been granted for a team of contractors to undertake a three-month clean-up of WWII material at Torokina, and at the time of writing it was anticipated that the team was expected to arrive in PNG to begin work in April 2010. The Office of Weapons Removal and Abatement has made it clear that the area of the former WWII base (about 120 square miles) is far too large and the terrain too difficult (it is largely covered in dense jungles, swamps, etc.) for the contractors to be able to hope to undertake a complete clearance of the area. Rather, it will aim to destroy most unexploded material already known to the local population and will train local police officers possibly to destroy some small items and to map finds of other bombs and weapons with a view to the contractors returning from time to time to destroy newly uncovered weaponry. It is anticipated that this mission will make a considerable contribution to reducing the extent of what is probably the single most significant source of additional weapons for combatant groups and criminal elements in Bougainville.

Weapons Disposal and Reconciliation

The developments discussed earlier in this chapter concerning the demilitarization of Bougainville detailed specific provisions of the 2001 Bougainville Peace Agreement in relation to several distinct issues, including weapons disposal. But as discussed in relation to the implementation of those arrangements, they in general related to the agreed weapons disposal plan set out in the peace agreement, which was implemented under the supervision of the UNOMB. With the departure of the UNOMB from mid-2005, that plan was regarded as completed, and yet it was well understood that there continued to be many weapons still in the hands of combatants and others. This fact was a matter of considerable concern to the ABG from the moment it took office, as were the closely associated issues of not only the many localized disputes that remained unresolved and unreconciled, but also the Me'ekamui government and the MDF which remained opposed to the peace process. It was widely acknowledged that these issues constituted significant obstacles to weapons disposal and to further progress in peacebuilding.

However, very soon after the ABG took office, a series of developments occurred that contributed to the emergence of complex localized conflict in the southern part of Bougainville. This conflict made the tasks for the ABG of developing realistic plans for weapons disposal and reconciliation far more difficult than had been expected. The ABG and its local and international partners did take a number of initiatives in this regard, but they did not appear to be making much progress. But beginning in August 2007, and gaining momentum in 2009–10, there has been considerable progress. Various elements of the increasingly factionalized Me'ekamui government and the MDF have developed working relationships with the ABG, localized reconciliation has moved forward, and elements of the MDF have begun seriously discussing disposing of their weapons.

These significant aspects of progress toward achieving important goals of the peace agreement cannot readily be discussed without first mentioning in brief the sources and main contours of the localized conflict that from late 2005 to 2009 appeared as having the potential to destabilize or even destroy the peace process. Those matters are discussed in chapter 6, which concludes with a brief assessment of not only the extent of progress toward disposal of the remaining weapons, reconciliation, and the engaging of "dissident" elements in the peace process, but also the question of whether the difficult experience of renewed conflict from late 2005 suggests shortcomings in the design, operation, and withdrawal of the main elements of the international intervention in support of the Bougainville peace process.

6

Ongoing Tension and Conflict, Progress in Weapons Disposal, and Reconciliation, 2005 to 2010

In the four-year period from the signing of the Bougainville Peace Agreement in August 2001 to the establishing of the ABG in June 2005, significant progress was made in the peace process. The latter date marked a critically important point. It involved the official "completion" of the weapons disposal process, the joint commencement of both the ABG and the 10- to 15-year timetable for the conduct of the referendum on independence, and the departure of the main visible element (the UN mission) of the international intervention. Paradoxically, these much anticipated developments in the peace process also heralded significant changes in conditions in Bougainville that, in retrospect, had the potential to exacerbate prior sources of tension and conflict. In particular

- for those supporting the peace process, expectations regarding what the ABG could accomplish were probably unrealistically high;
- for leaders and groups outside the process, the advent of a new Bougainville government was a source of grave concern for their long-term viability;
- for armed groups with tense relations with neighbors also holding weapons, there was deep uncertainty about what the departure of the UN and installment of the ABG with some powers over police might mean; and
- for the PNG government, there was also trepidation about whether secession might now be inevitable, although it has supported establishing the ABG.

That there should be such sources of tension and conflict in a post-conflict situation should not be a surprise. Despite agreements, diverse sources of tension and conflict usually tend to simmer, even once the main conflict is resolved—the previous intensity just finds new outlets.

In the Bougainville case, however, although none of the sources of tension and conflict was entirely new, in retrospect it is clear that in mid-2005 the dangers for the peace process either were not recognized or were underestimated.

As will be evident from the discussion in this chapter, at some points the dangers seemed so severe that the viability of the ongoing peace process appeared to be under threat, so much so that serious doubts could be raised about the wisdom of the departure of the PMG and the UNOMB. Yet by early 2010 the extent of the threat to the peace process appears to have diminished, the change being due for the most part to initiatives taken by Bougainvilleans.

Spoilers: Groups Outside the Process—Ona, Me'ekamui, and a New Royal Kingdom

From the time he announced his Republic of Me'ekamui in early 1998, Ona had been in a difficult position, opposing the peace process but unwilling to mount a military challenge his former associates and other leaders who supported the process. His constant public criticism of the peace process, intended in large part to both undermine it and encourage former supporters to return to him when (as he expected it would) the process faltered, was often quite unsettling for leaders who supported peace. This was particularly so at the points when serious difficulties arose during negotiations (for example, in late 2000 when an impasse concerning the referendum issue developed between the PNG government and the leadership of the Bougainville groups participating in the process).

Ona's position was not one of only declaration. At times it appeared that the armed MDF elements present in many communities were a serious risk to peace. Not only were they refusing to dispose of their weapons, but even in the years before 2005, some elements had used their weapons publicly in ways that destablized the peace and also contributed to localized conflict. Some examples suffice to underline this point.

First, as mentioned already in chapter 4, PMG vehicles were shot at several times, and it was widely assumed that MDF elements were involved. Second, the MDF mounted armed roadblocks, a permanent one from 1998 to the time of this writing at Morgan Junction (see chapter 3)—where the east coast trunk road and the only road into the Me'ekamui "no-go-zone" intersect—and another established for various periods from the late 1990s to about 2004 near Aropa, on the coastal trunk road between the former provincial capital (Arawa) and the southern town of Buin. Both roadblocks constituted significant restrictions on freedom of movement, and weapons were used to prevent access to members of opposing groups and to extract financial imposts and (sometimes) to steal goods from travelers. This was part of a broader pattern—two other armed roadblocks were established by separate MDF elements between 2005 and 2008, one at Tonu in Siwai and one at Ugubakobu in the Konnou area east of Buin Town (see later discussion about localized conflict in South Bougainville). (The locations of all four roadblocks are shown in Map 6.)

Third, as already mentioned in chapter 4, late in 2002 and early in 2003 a senior MDF commander from central Bougainville was widely believed to have instigated the theft of between 60 and 90 BRA and BRF weapons from PMG-supplied containers being used as part of the weapons disposal process. At the time, the theft gave rise to grave concerns about the possibility that Ona or the MDF, or both, might have been contemplating amassing a significant proportion of the total available weapons with a view to attempting an armed takeover of the government. This led to heightened tension between the BRA and MDF leaderships, and an armed clash at the Morgan Junction roadblock in mid-2003 left one MDF member killed and another injured. A significant proportion of the stolen weapons (though not all of them) was subsequently returned by the MDF. Fourth, at various points MDF elements have been involved in theft of vehicles used by the UNDP and other donors (although it is also the case that this has been part of a wider pattern in criminalized activities, sometimes involving former BRA members). Fifth, and finally, armed MDF elements played significant roles in the escalation of localized conflict in south Bougainville, as discussed a little later.

It must be emphasized here that the MDF was not necessarily acting on Ona's explicit orders in all or any of the instances just outlined. To a large degree it was merely part of yet another very loose localized groups and coalitions of groups and interests associated with Ona and the Me'ekamui government (see Map 6 for an indication of the extent of the areas where MDF units are located).

As discussed elsewhere in this monograph, when he originally opposed the peace process, Ona was probably reasonably confident that it would fail without his support—after all, he had been the preeminent figure in Bougainville politics since the late 1980s. But as the process moved forward to the 2001 political settlement, and its anticipated implementation, Ona felt increasingly marginalized. To make things more difficult for him, by 2002–03 many of the people in the "no-go-zone" were increasingly vocal about their dissatisfaction with the lack of basic services available there (including health and education). Many were seeking an end to the "no-go-zone," a proposal that Ona could not entertain, because it would have been tantamount to acknowledging the end of his claims as head of a separate government.

Instead, he sought new ways of reestablishing his political dominance. Of considerable importance here was the strange alliance that he developed in 2003 and 2004 with Noah Musingku, the operator of a fraudulent investment scheme (a Ponzi scheme), who is Bougainville's equivalent of U.S. financier Bernie Madoff, whose career ended in the courtroom in July 2009 when he was sentenced to 150 years imprisonment for defrauding investors of many billions of U.S. dollars. (Musingku's background and barely credible activities in Bougainville from 2003 are discussed in more detail below.) Ona and most of his strongest supporters were victims of Musingku's fraudulent scheme, something made possible by Ona's deep fear that the progress in the peace process was resulting in his losing legitimacy and popular support. As a result he was open to Musingku's promises of fabulous rates of return (100 percent interest per month) on investments that would enable Ona to fund restoration and development in Bougainville and payment of compensation to those whose property had been destroyed or family members killed or injured during the conflict. Ironically, Ona had significant sources of funds available, derived in particular from large amounts of gold that Ona was buying at quite low rates from alluvial gold miners operating in the "no-go-zone" (many of them panning gold in the tailings of the Panguna mine which had been disposed of by BCL between 1972 and 1989 by dumping them into a local river system).

Many of his supporters also had access to gold, while others had managed to reopen long dormant bank accounts after the peace process began, and in that way gained access to funds. Ona encouraged all of them to invest in Musingku's scheme.

It is probably a measure of the extent to which Ona was desperate to find new sources of legitimacy that he also was apparently persuaded by Musingku that the former Republic of Me'ekamui should be transformed into the Royal Kingdom of Me'ekamui, with Ona crowned as its new monarch in May 2004. Musingku was also crowned at the same time as prince of a separate but related Kingdom of Papala (a strange development discussed further, below). Musingku seems to have been supported in these monarchical endeavors by shadowy figures from Australia and England whom he brought to Bougainville in 2004. In fact, Ona's alliance with Msuingku, the pressure he applied to his supporters to invest funds with Musingku on which they received no return, and his purported coronation all undermined Ona's credibility in Bougainville generally and especially among his own supporters and key advisers.[1] The growing criticisms being made by such advisers was one of several factors that led Ona to dismiss or suspend several of them in the second half of 2004, a move that was in turn to become a contributing factor in significant divisions in the Me'ekamui government that emerged following Ona's death in July 2005. Among those dismissed was the long-serving "general" of the MDF, Moses Pipiro, whom Ona replaced late in 2004 with Chris Uma, the head of the MDF elements that operated the armed roadblock at the Morgan Junction.

Ona's concern about the threat to his credibility as a key leader in Bougainville posed by ongoing progress in the peace process was also evident in other actions he took in the lead-up to the first general elections for the ABG in May 2005. Ona held several public rallies in the main urban centers of Bougainville, attacking the elections and making wild claims about the Kingdom of Me'ekamui and the huge funds that he would soon have available to provide services in and reconstruction for Bougainville. These were the only forays that Ona ever made into

1. Despite Musingku's claims, there is no evidence of any history of monarchical rule in Bougainville or of extensive states of any kind. Social groups in all of Bougainville's language groups are in general small and highly autonomous.

direct political competition with leaders supporting the peace process. His almost incomprehensible statements at rallies made him a curiosity, and his claims were not treated seriously—indeed, they further undermined his already eroded credibility. He had little or no impact on the ABG elections.

Then in July 2005, quite unexpectedly, just a few weeks after the elections, Ona died in his home village of Guava in the "no-go-zone." The cause of his death was (and still is) a matter of intense speculation in Bougainville, with talk of murder (by magic or poison) and various kinds of illness. As there was no autopsy, the speculation can be expected to continue. But close advisers to Ona at the time of his death believe that in large part it was the result of stress that they link directly to two main factors. One was his realization in the last months of his life that he had been misled by Musingku—that neither the monies he and his supporters had invested nor the promised fabulous returns on the investment would ever be paid. The other was the dispute that he had been having with his former advisers whom he had dismissed or suspended in late 2004.

From Spoilers to Participants in the Process: Me'ekamui Factions

In the months leading up to and immediately after Ona's death, the leadership of the Me'ekamui government and the MDF was in disarray. The leaders whom Ona had dismissed or suspended were not forgiven, neither by Ona's immediate family nor other key leaders who had remained close to Ona, such as Chris Uma (the loyalists). Over the next few months a struggle for credibility and legitimacy developed between the two groups, each claiming to be the true Me'ekamui government. (The struggle was further confused because Musingku also claimed to be the true inheritor of Ona's authority, through the government of his Kingdom of Papala, but for the most part those claims were given little credence in the "no-go-zone.") The leaders who had been dismissed or suspended by Ona were based together in the Panguna area, around the previous headquarters of the mining operation, whereas the loyalists were much more scattered (some at Ona's home village of Guava, a few kilometers from Panguna, some about 20 kilometers away in Arawa and at the Morgan Junction, others in Buka and elsewhere in Bougainville), thus making it difficult for them to take unified positions.

Ona's death had created space for more open discussion among communities in the "no-go-zone" about the conditions in which they lived (generally lacking in basic government services and with freedom of movement into and out of the area considerably restricted by the Morgan Junction roadblock). By 2006 there was more open discussion of the need for restoration of government services and freedom of movement for the "no-go-zone" than had been possible when Ona was alive. The Panguna-based "dissident" leaders included some who had maintained links with Joseph Kabui, the president of the ABG, and in 2006 they opened dialogue with him through one of the two Catholic Church bishops of Bougainville. With encouragement from the bishops and other mediating figures, the dissident leaders saw the opportunity of gaining popular support from the population of the "no-go-zone" by restoring services; as a result in August 2007 they signed the Panguna Communiqué with the ABG. The dissident leaders entered that agreement under the name "Me'ekamui Government of Unity (MGU)." The Panguna Communiqué provided for restoring services by establishing a Panguna district administration under the joint authority of the ABG and the MGU, for "healing political differences," for moving toward weapons containment, for "dismantling" the Morgan Junction roadblock, and for involvement of the people of the "no-go-zone" in any discussions of the future of the Panguna mine. By entering into such arrangements, the dissident Me'ekamui leadership effectively agreed to join the peace process.

The Panguna district office was established late in 2007, and since then government services have very slowly begun to be delivered into the former "no-go-zone," with progress being limited to some degree by the Morgan Junction roadblock, which continues to operate under the direction of Ona loyalist Chris Uma. Together with other loyalists, he claims to be part of the original Me'ekamui government and that MGU leaders have no right to use the term "Me'ekamui" as part of the name of their organization. At the same time, the strong community support for the district office and the restoration of services has made it impossible for Uma and his MDF supporters at the roadblock to prevent government officers and AusAID road contractors from entering the "no-go-zone." However, they do sometimes turn back officials or visitors at the roadblock, usually as a way of emphasizing that they too have a role and should be recognized and consulted.

Curiously, though AusAID-funded road contractors have had no difficulty getting Uma's agreement to move back and forth through the roadblock, none of AusAID's own officials based in Bougainville or visiting from Port Moresby has been into the "no-go-zone," because the Australian Department of Foreign Affairs and Trade has opposed their seeking permission from Uma to do so, on the basis that this would give recognition, credibility, and status to Uma. As a result, through April 2010, AusAID personnel have not been able to assess the situation of the perhaps 10,000 people living in the "no-go-zone," many of whom live in very poor conditions without proper housing (houses were burned by the PNG forces in 1989–90) and basic services (even immunization services) for almost 20 years. Yet this refusal to engage with Uma seems to be contrary to much of what had been learned earlier in the Bougainville peace process about the advantages of engaging with all parties and factions to the extent possible.

The importance of that very lesson was unexpectedly underlined in a graphic manner in March 2010. Consultations were undertaken by a team of ABG officials with communities of landowners of the areas covered by the BCL mining-related leases about how they might organize themselves to be represented in possible future processes to review the Panguna mining agreements (the Bougainville Copper Agreement—BCA). These consultations led to the first detailed discussions ever to have occurred between the ABG officials and Chris Uma and other senior members of the original Me'ekamui government. Among other things, it became clear that Uma and the other leaders wanted to be part of any process of review of the BCA, as spokespersons for those opposed to mining. Discussion of such issues eventually led to agreement that the ABG officials would report on their consultations to a joint meeting in Buka Town of the ABG together with representatives of the MGU and the original Me'ekamui government. That meeting took place on March 17, 2010, and ultimately resulted in a memorandum of understanding (MOU) being signed between representatives of the three entities to continue discussion about the BCA review process, issues about establishing local government based strongly on traditional authority, reconciling long-standing differences between the MDF and other former combatant groups, working toward criminal amnesty and other arrangements needed to support weapons disposal, and other practical steps needed to achieve unity among the three entities.

At the time of this writing, it is too early to assess the full significance of the March 2010 MOU, for it involves little more than a commitment to continue talking, and it is not yet clear how far that process will develop. At this stage perhaps its main significance lies in the fact that it represented the first time the three groups had met together and, in particular, the first, that Uma and the Ona loyalists in the original Me'ekamui government had engaged with the ABG leaders. They effectively appeared to be entering into the peace process, even if only tentatively.

Spoilers: Groups outside the Process—Musingku and the Royal Kingdom of Papala

Noah Musingku, a Bougainvillean from Siwai in southwest Bougainville, is the founder and director of U-Vistract, a failed Ponzi scheme involving affinity fraud (that is fraud based on exploitation of an affinity between the perpetrator and the victims). The scheme began operating in Bougainville in 1997 and in the PNG capital (Port Moresby) in July 1998, with Musingku claiming he wished to assist Bougainvilleans and Pentecostal Christians all over PNG by offering them 100 percent interest per month on investments, which he said he could deliver because of his secret investment methods associated with his development of a new world financial system. He greatly enhanced his legitimacy in the eyes of investors by offering complex rationales for his scheme based on long-standing Bougainville custom and Christian principles and conspicuously using modern technology (computers, satellite dishes, satellite phones, and so on), which gave the appearance of competence and professionalism—especially winning in postconflict Bougainville where not even the provincial government had access to such resources. Even more important, of course, Musingku also delivered the promised returns to selected investors—but in common with all Ponzi schemes, these came, not through any secret investment method, but rather from funds received from new investors. Beginning in July 1998, U-Vistract had sought investments in most PNG urban centers, and all parts of Bougainville, as well as in Australia and Fiji. The scheme was reported to have attracted investments of PNGK521 million (about US$ 175 million) before it was officially liquidated early in 2000 by legal action taken by the PNG central bank as a result of complaints made by unpaid investors. Musingku, however, ignored legal actions brought against him and continued to seek funds from investors.

In 2003 he evaded arrest under PNG law for contempt of court (in relation to court orders made in liquidation proceedings against U-Vistract) by relocating to the Me'ekamui "no-go-zone." He won Ona's support and protection of the MDF by promising the wealth that Ona was convinced he needed to restore his own preeminence in Bougainville. He also gained protection from the tens of thousands of unpaid investors in Bougainville from the 1997–2000 period. And he continued to find new investors, including Ona, in the "no-go-zone" and other parts of Bougainville, because he spouted a flood of stories about how the PNG and Australian governments, the World Bank, the ABG, and many other alleged culprits were in fear of his new economic system and wrongly blocking his access to the funds he needed to make immediate payouts of all funds invested together with the promised interest backdated to the date of original investment.

Musingku had a major falling out with Ona late in 2004 after which he moved to his home area of Tonu, Siwai. There he built on claims that he had been developing while with Ona, to the effect that he was heading the government of yet another independent monarchical state—the Royal Kingdom of Papala, which, he said, was involved in a partnership with Ona's Royal Kingdom of Me'ekamui. It is widely reported in Bougainville that Ona and Musingku signed an agreement called the "twin kingdoms agreement" in which they promised to recognize one another's royal credentials and to work together. During 2004 Musingku gave several speeches (written copies of which he distributed widely in Bougainville) in which he drew on information technology metaphors, explaining that the twin kingdoms concept involved the Kingdom of Papala as the "software" that worked in concert with the "hardware" represented by Ona's Kingdom of Me'ekamui.

After Ona's death, Musingku claimed that the twin kingdoms had now merged, and that in a visit he had received from Ona shortly before the latter's death, Ona had handed his authority to Musingku. As a result, he said, his Kingdom of Papala was now the true Me'ekamui government. While this claim had little if any impact in the "no-go-zone," it helped maintain limited local support for Musingku in the Siwai area of southwest Bougainville, where he had based himself in late 2004. From the time of his arrival there he used local armed MDF elements to provide security, calling them "royal guards" or "palace guards." Apparently encouraged by their new status, these "security" forces became involved in local crime and conflict. In 2006, several people were injured or killed in armed clashes with police and with other armed groups in the area. The MDF also mounted a roadblock at Tonu, apparently originally to help ensure Musingku's security, but which contributed further to the lack of freedom of movement as had other MDF roadblocks at Morgan Junction and Ugabakobu.

That the Bougainville communities in and around Tonu harbored Musingku is not surprising. To such rural communities, the modern state is remote, and people living a largely subsistence lifestyle, often with little or no formal education, can find alternative explanations of the state and the economy a powerful message, especially when accompanied by promises of significant financial returns, all apparently based in both Bougainvillean custom and Christian principles, bolstered by continual "flaunting" of heavy reliance on modern technology.

In another move probably driven by concern for his own security, in late 2005 Musingku announced the engaging of five former soldiers (commandos) from Fiji to provide training to young men who were to become security guards for his new international banking system. Musingku engaged the Fijians through Pentecostal Christian contacts in Fiji through whom he had earlier raised several million dollars in investments. He offered the former soldiers US$ 1.5 million each for a year's service. Four of the five who later left Musingku reported that the proposition of working to assist a Christian banker in Bougainville seemed very attractive when compared to the alternative employment then on offer to them—working with security firms in Iraq!

To Bougainvillean and PNG authorities, however, the picture was quite different. Musingku appeared to be a serious threat to peace and security. Together, his claims to head a new government, the violent activities of the MDF elements associated with him, and his hiring of what were regarded as Fijian mercenaries were seen as possibly indicating intentions to overthrow the ABG. By late 2006 concern grew about what seemed a seriously deteriorating security situation in south Bougainville involving not just Musingku but also other groups (see the discussion below about localized conflict).

In late November 2006 a group of former combatants (BRA and BRF) calling themselves the Bougainville Freedom Fighters, accompanied by some police officers, attacked Musingku's headquarters with a view to capturing Musingku and the five Fijians (by then believed to have committed immigration offenses when they entered PNG in 2005 on missionary visas, as well as offenses related to training illegal armed forces). One of the attackers was killed, and several people on both sides (including Musingku) were injured. In the aftermath, four of the five Fijians, by then in fear for their own safety and increasingly aware that it was unlikely that they would receive the remuneration promised by Musingku, were contacted by a local Catholic priest who was himself a Fijian, and early in 2007 they were persuaded to surrender to the police.

At the time of this writing, Musingku's credibility has been severely damaged by his Ponzi scheme and exaggerated claims. He remains in Tonu, with one of the Fijian former soldiers, still supported by armed elements (local MDF and others) and claiming that he will make repayments shortly. In July 2009 it was reported that he would do this by issuing his own currency—the "Bougainville kina," which, according to one follower, bears various images of Jesus Christ, Musingku, and some of his relations, as well as Bougainville's late president, Joseph Kabui.[2]

Musingku has had a number of negative impacts, contributing to tensions and conflict in Bougainville. In particular, his fraudulent scheme has sucked a large amount of money out of productive activities. In his alliance with Ona in 2003–4, his claims reduced pressure that might otherwise have pushed Ona and/or his followers to support the

2. "U-Vistract Conman Offers 'Jesus Money,'" *Sydney Morning Herald*, July 8, 2009.

peace process. From late 2004 to the time of this writing, his activities in Tonu, southwest Bougainville, have contributed significantly to the localized violent conflict there and to general instability.

Localized Conflict in South Bougainville

The localized conflict in south Bougainville that began in late 2005 has already been touched on. There is a long history of both tensions and conflict in southern Bougainville, and this helps to explain why many of the local conflicts from the 1992 to 1997 period have proved difficult to resolve even now, despite many reconciliation efforts in Bougainville since the early 1990s, and especially since 1997. In general, reconciliation programs seem to have been less successful in south Bougainville than in central and northern areas. However, despite this, from the time when the peace process began in 1997 until 2005, for the most part the localized conflict in south Bougainville ceased.

Before discussing a little more of the origins and impacts of this local conflict, it must be emphasized that while armed conflict was involved, it did not represent a resumption of the main dimensions of the conflict that had devastated Bougainville between 1988 and 1997. First, it did not involve conflict between PNG and Bougainville forces, and second, it did not involve conflict between the two main Bougainville protagonists of the earlier period (the BRA and the BRF). On the other hand, it did involve very localized conflicts, which in some instances were connected with unreconciled disputes and conflicts that occurred in the earlier period.

The localized conflict in question has occurred mainly in the adjoining Siwai and Buin areas of south Bougainville, which were embroiled in complex tensions well before the Bougainville conflict began. The areas have dense populations compared to most other parts of Bougainville and had experienced increasing levels of land disputes and economic and social conflict related to distribution of increasingly scarce land resources and economic opportunities. This history probably was a significant reason why there was particularly bitter localized conflict in these areas during the main period of internal conflict in Bougainville (1990–97) and why, after the peace process had begun in 1997, there was limited progress (when compared to other parts of Bougainville) in achieving reconciliation in relation to the localized conflict.

The limited economic development in south Bougainville since the end of the conflict in 1997 has been a factor contributing to ongoing tensions. For instance, while major investment in the cocoa industry since the late 1990s saw cocoa production by small farmers rise dramatically in north Bougainville, production levels were not particularly good in central Bougainville and worse in the south.[3] Anecdotal evidence suggests that higher rainfall levels evident in south Bougainville from about the late 1990s interfered with the setting of cocoa flowers, resulting in much lower production levels there than before the conflict. Without a significant alternative crop, there have been restricted opportunities for earning cash income in the south compared to elsewhere in Bougainville. This has resulted in significant levels of migration from Siwai and Buin to other parts of Bougainville.

While local conflicts were muted during the peace negotiations, there were a few notable exceptions, in particular relating to an intra-BRA conflict in the Buin area, which requires brief mention because it became a significant factor in the localized conflict from late 2005. Conflict between BRA elements in the area around Buin Town erupted late in 1998, when a senior BRA commander was killed by a BRA unit commanded by a close relative of the deceased. That death sparked a series of armed clashes between the surviving commander and yet another BRA element from the Konnou area, some distance east of Buin Town, that had been associated with the deceased commander. Several people were injured in those clashes, between 1998 and 2001, and repeated reconciliation efforts failed to resolve the conflict.[4] From around 2003 the leader of the BRA element east of Buin sought to improve his security by developing links with the MDF, a development that played a role in the further conflict discussed later here. (The surviving commander from near Buin Town was later a key figure in organizing the Bougainville Freedom Fighters group, which attacked

3. Scales, Craemer, and Thappa, *Market Chain Development in Peacebuilding.*

4. A brief account of the original killing, its consequences, and some early (though actually unsuccessful) reconciliation efforts can be found in Howley, *Breaking Spears*, 106–09.

Musingku's headquarters in November 2006, armed with modern weapons that the commander had contained as part of the UN-supervised disarmament process, but had refused to destroy, in large part because of the ongoing intra-BRA conflict in which he was involved.)

Between 1998 and 2005, it seems that the general commitment to peace by communities all over Bougainville together with the presence of the international intervention had a significant impact on reducing localized conflict in south Bougainville, but not enough to reduce the likelihood of such conflict resuming. Without the kind of effective reconciliation that was happening elsewhere in Bougainville, however, it is perhaps not surprising that localized conflict resumed in the south, nor that, for the most part, it resumed after the departure of the UN mission in mid-2005. The resumption of localized conflict was related to the availability of numerous weapons in south Bougainville. An unknown but significant part of the total MDF weapons (which were not contained as part of the UNOMB supervised weapons disposal process, 2001–5) were held by MDF elements in south and southwest Bougainville. Informal arrangements for loan, transfer, and even trade of weapons among MDF groups meant that when tensions occurred in the south, additional MDF weapons tended to move there. Some BRA and BRF groups in south Bougainville also retained weapons. It is also likely that some weapons were traded into south Bougainville from neighboring Solomon Islands after serious internal conflict there from 1999 resulted in many weapons being lost or stolen from police armories. Finally, from about 2006, increasing amounts of World War II weapons and ammunition were becoming available from Torokina, and armed groups in the south were getting access to the funds needed to buy such weapons because of revenue collected at roadblocks and involvement of some MDF and other armed groups in small-scale gold mining.

Until mid-2005 the presence of the international intervention had been a significant factor encouraging BRA and BRF groups to support the peace process and to put aside their weapons. From 1997 to 2005 any use of a weapon in conflict by a member of those groups could involve a ceasefire violation, with accountability to the TMG, PMG, or UN mission usually taken seriously. In addition, those groups came under intense pressure to dispose of their weapons during the disarmament process. The presence of the UN mission was even a source of indirect pressure on the Me'ekamui government and the MDF to refrain from violence. With the departure of the UN, such pressures on groups retaining weapons were removed. Further, any group aggrieved by use of weapons by a neighboring group could no longer seek redress or protection by complaining to a neutral body, making self-help a more significant option when trouble occurred.

It must also be noted that the role of the ABG and the police in south Bougainville, which was virtually nonexistent from 1989 to 1997, has continued to be quite limited since the peace process began, even in areas where there has not been an MDF presence. Although basic services (education and health) have been partially restored in Siwai and Buin, ABG administrative offices and police posts are few. In general, the ability of the police to control law and order is quite limited in most parts of Bougainville, but especially in the south. For the most part, since the implementation of the Bougainville Peace Agreement began late in 2001, police personnel have not been permitted to carry weapons. In areas where they do operate reasonably effectively (mainly in parts of north and central Bougainville), they rely mainly on community support. In south Bougainville, such cooperation continues to be more limited in many areas.

Some incidents involved in the development of local conflict in the Siwai and Buin areas have already been touched on. They include the involvement of the MDF elements associated with Musingku in local conflict in Siwai, some involving payback related to past conflict, and some involving criminal activities. Others involved the above-mentioned former BRA elements in the Konnou area, east of Buin Town, that clashed with close relatives who had been part of BRF elements that had split from the BRA in the midst of bitter local conflict in the 1992–95 period. Another involved the Bougainville Freedom Fighters' attack on Musingku's headquarters at Tonu. Still others involved the Siwai and Konnou MDF elements setting up armed roadblocks that—like other MDF roadblocks already mentioned—restricted freedom of movement and became involved in criminal activities.

These were just a few of a number of starting points that eventually saw about 10 distinct armed groups operating in south Bougainville by

2007–08 and engaging in localised conflict that contributed to over 60 deaths in the period from late 2005 to 2009. The number of weapons in the hands of the armed groups was growing as a result of trade with elements of the MDF, as well as the former BRA and BRF elsewhere in Bougainville, and also because of weapons flowing from the former United States and Australian World War II base at Torokina. The situation seemed bleak.

However, during 2007 and the first half of 2008, growing concern across Bougainville about the dangers of the escalating conflict had pushed the ABG, churches, local governments, and community groups of all kinds, with support from donors (UNDP, AusAID, and NZAID) to put a great deal of effort into persuading those involved in the escalating localized conflict to reconcile. The efforts by a range of local community leaders (chiefs, clan leaders, leaders of local women's organizations, local church leaders, and others) were particularly important, often involving senior leaders from local communities walking into the "camps" of opposing factions, talking to their leaders, and encouraging them to cease using firearms and seek to understand the fears and concerns of their opponents. The ABG established a task force to work on local reconciliation in 2008 and an office of peace and reconciliation in 2009, and these bodies offered limited funding and other support to these local efforts. Beginning in about mid-2008 these efforts began to bear fruit, assisted by the growing concern also among some of the groups involved in the conflict about the serious dangers posed for them if the escalating conflict were not contained. Leaders of some of those groups began to exercise restraint and explore ways to end the conflict. The work of the local community leaders to encourage an end to the local conflict continues at the time of this writing.

In December 2008 such efforts received a significant boost with the election of James Tanis as the new ABG president. He replaced the first ABG president, Joseph Kabui, who had died in June 2008 and who had also strongly supported efforts to achieve peace in the south. Tanis had an advantage in that he was a younger man who was a former BRA member, and he had maintained communication with key MDF leaders and was in a good position to talk directly to some leaders of armed groups in south Bougainville, including Musingku, with whom Tanis had attended high school in the 1980s. In February 2009 Tanis spent two days with Musingku at Tonu, and among other things discussed with him the necessity for ensuring that local armed conflict did not resume and the need for disposing of the weapons held by the MDF elements associated with Musingku. Tanis also discussed publicly the possibility of some form of pardon for Musingku, which did not sit well with many Bougainvilleans who believe that Musingku should be made to account for his fraudulent activities. Tanis also held discussions with other leaders of armed groups in south Bougainville and leaders of the MDF elements associated with the original Me'ekamui government. These efforts contributed to the extensive peacebuilding efforts made by local leaders in south Bougainville by much reducing the likelihood of any support flowing to MDF elements in south Bougainville from the MDF elements led by Chris Uma in central Bougainville. All of these factors together contributed to reducing tensions and violence in 2009, and the progress appeared to continue early in 2010. Former Bougainville governor John Momis, by now a candidate for the post of president in the second ABG general election[5], contributed to the effort and was reported to be working closely with leaders of MDF elements in the Konnou area east of Buin Town, encouraging them to lay down their weapons and support the peace process.

Relations between Bougainville and the PNG Government

In general, relations between Bougainville and the PNG government have been reasonable in the period from June 2005 to early 2010, although with some tense periods. There is still considerable mistrust of PNG on the part of some key former BRA and BIG leaders, some within and some outside the ABG. Such elements tend to interpret any suggestion of delay by the PNG government in implementation of any

5. As this book was being prepared for publication in June 2010, final results for the second ABG election were announced. John Momis was elected president, receiving 52.35 percent of the vote, with James Tanis coming second, with just under 21 percent. Of the 39 other members of the Bougainville legislature, more than 75 percent of the sitting members lost their seats. Voting proceeded smoothly in all areas, with no interference from any of the roadblocks or any of the armed groups in the south of Bougainville.

aspect of the peace agreement (for example, related to complexities in the process of transfer of functions and powers or failure to pay the Restoration and Development Grant under the 2010 PNG budget) as evidence of bad faith on the part of PNG. On the PNG side, there are elements in the bureaucracy as well as elected leaders who fear that leadership in Bougainville is already committed to secession, so that there seems little point in making major efforts to implement the agreement, which, they believe, would just assist the progress to separation.

In some ways, neither side has entirely grasped the inherent logic of the combination of a high level of autonomy for Bougainville coupled with a referendum on independence deferred for a period of years after the autonomy arrangements begin to operate. The logic is that in the 10 to 15 years from the establishment of the ABG in 2005, the PNG government has the opportunity to work closely with the ABG to promote all forms of development in Bougainville in a way that could be expected to encourage Bougainvilleans to consider the possible merits of remaining a part of PNG when it comes time to vote in the referendum. Unless both sides share that approach to the agreement's implementation, there is a strong likelihood of increasing tensions as the date for holding the referendum approaches.

Ongoing Efforts in Support of Unification, Reconciliation, and Weapons Disposal

Efforts in pursuit of peace need to continue in order to ensure that three major threats to peace and security are resolved. The first threat is armed groups that oppose the peace process; work must continue to bring unity among all major groups in Bougainville. As long as armed groups that oppose the peace process exist, there is the risk of armed conflict emerging again. This threat needs to be dealt with by ongoing efforts to engage with groups that do not support the peace process. In this regard, the developments just discussed in relation to the ABG engaging with the MGU and the original Me'ekamui government are seen as significant.

The second threat is the unresolved localized conflicts, some originating from before the Bougainville conflict began (1988) and others from incidents that occurred during the conflict (1988–97) or since the peace process begun. It is widely accepted among Bougainville leaders that a great deal of effort needs to be made to encourage local reconciliation. The ABG's peace and reconciliation office has been established with this goal in mind, and although it is very small and has very limited resources, it is working closely with local NGOs and the UNDP to identify local disputes where reconciliation is required and providing support to encourage local reconciliation. Some observers are growing concerned, however, that the ABG, and donors such as the UNDP, are not being sufficiently careful in the support being provided to local reconciliation efforts, and are getting to the stage where they are not merely funding such things as costs of mediation and transport, but are allegedly funding even the pigs and customary shell money used to provide compensation or restore balance in reciprocal relationships damaged by conflict. If true, the danger here is that such financial arrangements could devalue the largely customary reconciliation processes, dramatically devaluing their efficacy. Early in 2010 the picture here is far from clear and probably requires careful evaluation.

The third threat is the continued widespread availability of weapons in Bougainville, and their availability for use by armed groups (MDF and others) as well as by criminals, businesspeople, and others in the community. Since the end of the UNOMB-supervised weapons disposal program in mid-2005, there have been some limited weapons disposal efforts. For example, the New Zealand ambassador funded ad hoc arrangements from 2005 under which 12 or 15 weapons were destroyed in return for the weapon holders receiving training of one kind or another. Further, a few other weapons have been destroyed or handed to local police officers as part of local reconciliation ceremonies. Late in 2007 the ABG declared 2008 its official "year of reconciliation and weapons disposal," a response to growing concern about difficulties in making progress toward these related twin goals. The UNDP provided support with a consultant's report on weapons disposal. But overall no real progress toward a more generalized solution to the weapons disposal problem was made in 2008. In 2009 the UNDP provided yet another consultant's report, this one focused on what it identified as a need to empower communities to develop the capacity to encourage holders of weapons to give them up. However, the report did not not suggest concrete approaches for developing such programs that might lead to the main armed groups (MDF and others) disposing of weapons.

There are some signs of early progress in having armed MDF elements and other armed groups dispose of weapons, however. For example, the MDF elements associated with the MGU, in the Panguna area, began developing a weapons disposal program late in 2009, one that was still under local discussion early in 2010. Further, the MOU signed by the ABG, the MGU, and the original Me'ekamui government on March 17, 2010, mentioned the "need for an amnesty and pardon arrangement to support new weapons disposal programs," indicating an awareness on the part of all concerned of the need for multifaceted efforts to develop agreed-upon weapons disposal programs. Much more effort is going to be required from leaders of all factions before such programs can be developed and implemented.

Shortcomings in the International Intervention?

The obvious question arising from developments since 2005 already outlined in this chapter, and especially from the armed localized conflict in south Bougainville, is whether there were serious shortcomings in the way that the international intervention operated. To examine this, we can consider three closely related and obvious questions. First, does the extensive use of weapons suggest that the disarmament process was handled wrongly? Second, does the localized conflict since 2005 suggest that the PMG or the UN mission, or both, departed Bougainville too early? Third, was the Australian government correct in its assessment in 2003 that growing dependence of Bougainville leadership on the international intervention undermined the sustainability of the peace process?

Concerning the first question, it is now clear that key assumptions made during the implementation of the weapons disposal process were incorrect. In particular, the views articulated in July 2003 by the UN mission's director about the ways in which weapons not included in the disposal process could be dealt with were clearly incorrect. At the same time, however, it must be recalled that both the key Bougainville leaders supporting the peace process and the PNG government concurred with that assessment. Further, it is difficult to see how the disposal process could have been handled in such a way as to ensure a much more complete disposal of weapons, particularly given the refusal of the MDF to participate in the process at that time. It must also be remembered that some of the weapons coming into circulation since 2005 have been World War II weapons from Torokina. Surprisingly, it seems that during the weapons disposal process (2001–05), no one paid attention to the risks of renewed efforts to retrieve such weapons as has occurred since 2006. In large part this oversight can be explained by the fact that it was mainly BRA members who had access to limited numbers of World War II weapons during the conflict, and BRA leaders had not realized there were significant numbers of additional WWII weapons remaining undiscovered. They too were surprised by the large number of weapons found since 2006, as outlined earlier in this monograph.

Another way of handling the situation in order to assist in dealing with the increasing use of weapons in localized conflict would have been to have a more open-ended timeframe for departure of the PMG and the UN mission. As discussed in chapter 4, the Bougainville leaders involved in the peace process very much wanted the PMG to remain longer in 2003, in part to further support the agreed weapons disposal program. But there was no such pressure on the UN in mid-2005, largely because ABG leaders by then felt reasonably confident that they could manage the next stages of reconciliation and weapons disposal. Hence, to be realistic, because most leaders by 2005 believed there was little likelihood that the conflict would resume, it seems unlikely that a more open-ended departure date for either the PMG or the UN intervention would have been agreed to by those leaders. Moreover the Australian government would never have accepted such a proposal, there having been considerable difficulty in convincing Australian government entities even had to be convinced to keep the PMG in Bougainville to mid-2003.

Concerning the second question, in retrospect, it seems that the likelihood of localized conflict emerging after departure of the UN mission should have been anticipated. South Bougainville had a history of localized conflict from at least the early 1990s and of some armed clashes even during the peace process (1998–2001). Even Bougainville leaders supporting the peace process did not expect conflict to reemerge so it is difficult to be critical of the international community in that regard. More generally, at the time of this writing, Bougainville leaders appear to be managing the local situation in the south reasonably well. Apart from the November 2006 attack on Musingku's headquarters, the peace process has been maintained, without a return to sustained attempts to use force as a means of ending the localized conflict.

On the other hand, the experience since late 2005 does suggest that there may perhaps be a downside to the kind of "light footprint" international intervention used in Bougainville. Perhaps with more flexibility on the part of the intervention, ensuing problems could have more readily been dealt with. For example, after departure in 2003 the PMG regional forces could perhaps have kept a "watching brief" and maintained a capacity to return to support ongoing or new weapons disposal efforts. Even public discussion of the possibility of such a return would probably have acted as a considerable disincentive for groups prone to getting involved in localized conflict. If a small force had been available to work with the ABG, it could perhaps have provided breathing room as the local conflict emerged in late 2005. The pressure for armed action by former combatants against Musingku and the Fiji mercenaries would then have been much less. That alone would have been a significant contribution, for the attack on Musingku's headquarters involved armed action against MDF elements widely perceived as supported by the ABG. It was action that could easily have sparked a resumption of wider conflict.

Concerning the third question (the correctness, or otherwise, of the Australian government's 2003 assessment that Bougainvillean dependence on the international intervention could undermine the sustainability of the peace process), in retrospect there was some validity to that view. Not only were the leaders becoming heavily dependent on the PMG and the UNOMB for transport (usually by helicopter) to meetings, there was a growing reliance on UN and PMG personnel to mediate any significant interaction between Bougainville and PNG. With the departure of the PMG and the UN, while there have undoubtedly sometimes been difficulties in relations between the PNG and the ABG, in general, answers have been found. Moreover, there has been some gradual progress toward the ABG engaging with the main Bougainville factions that had remained outside the peace process, in the form of the Panguna Communiqué of August 2007 and the MOU of March 17, 2010. Through these and related steps, Bougainvilleans have continued to take on the ownership and control of the peace process that might well have ultimately been undermined had the main elements of the international intervention (the PMG and the UNOMB) remained much longer in Bougainville.

7

Twenty-Five Lessons from the International Peacebuilding Intervention

While it is not possible to simply transfer successful approaches from one international peacebuilding intervention to another where the context is quite different, it may still be helpful to understand key aspects of the dynamics that contributed to, and outcomes achieved by, a specific "light footprint" intervention that clearly had positive impacts for the peace process it supported. Such "lessons" may still be useful in terms of insights and points of reference for those planning interventions in different contexts.

For convenience, such possible lessons derived from the Bougainville experience are presented here in five broad but overlapping categories:

1. Understanding the context in which the conflict and subsequent peacebuilding intervention occurs.
2. Dealing with a conflict involving loose coalitions rather than defined parties.
3. Encouraging and supporting local processes.
4. Aspects of organizing and managing an international peacebuilding intervention.
5. Problems in managing the impacts of the funding of local activities and the state-building aspects of an intervention.

While many such lessons could be regarded as so obvious as to involve truisms, in practice they are often ignored. For that reason alone, what has been learned in an intervention, where their significance has been clearly underlined, is worthy of discussion.

Understanding the Context in Which Conflict and the Peacebuilding Intervention Occurs

The first category of lessons involves the extent to which the Bougainville case illustrates the need for those planning and managing an international intervention to understand the context in which the conflict and peace process occur. The discussion illuminates some of the possibilities, as well as limitations, arising from the particular context of the Bougainville conflict and peace process.

The Importance of Context

A peacebuilding intervention should be informed by a deep understanding of the context of the conflict and peace process.

A critically important factor not always readily taken into account in planning and implementing peacebuilding interventions is the need for understanding the local context of the conflict and peace process in question. By "context" I mean the geopolitical, cultural, economic, historic, and other factors that may shape the situation in which both the conflict and the peace process take place and that may also determine their outcomes. Without building a deep understanding of the context into analyses and strategies, no actor—local or international—can realistically expect to contribute constructively to the design and implementation of conflict resolution or peacebuilding processes appropriate to the situation. But whereas local actors tend to have at least some understanding of local context (although, of course, there may be all sorts of factors that make it hard for them to base their analyses and strategies on that understanding), it can be much more difficult for actors in the international community to develop and make use of such understanding.

In Bougainville many contextual factors shaped the way the conflict and peace process developed. While it would be easy to focus solely on the impact of the Panguna mine as the cause of the conflict, in fact many other and more complex factors were involved. They included Bougainville's geographic situation as an isolated, largely self-contained unit, with close links to one of PNG's neighbors, and with internal divisions arising from both sociolinguistic diversity, growing economic inequality, and rapid social change. Such factors contributed to both internal conflict among Bougainvilleans and problems in managing the peace process.

More generally, in any postconflict situation where new governmental and political structures are being developed, the stakes for political leadership are likely to be high. Where ethnic and similar divisions are strong, there will often be significant pressure on local leadership elements to seek advantage for particular communities or parts of communities. In such circumstances, if international community involvement in planning for or participating in actual state-building or constitutional engineering activities is not to run severe risks of being counterproductive, it needs to be based on good analysis of context.

An essential concomitant of the importance of context is the need for any international peacebuilding intervention to make use of a strong capacity to understand context from the earliest stages of planning the intervention and throughout its operation, an issue discussed later in this chapter.

Culture—A Significant Part of Context

Culture can be a vitally important aspect of the context, essential to an understanding of both the origins of the conflict and the dynamics of the peace process.

The importance of culture as an aspect of context of not just conflict but also peacebuilding needs to be emphasized. There is extensive literature on culture and conflict, most concerning interstate rather than intrastate conflict. While such literature often makes brief mention of the importance of culture in determining how conflict is understood, the form that it takes, and so on,[1] the focus tends to be on the need to understand and take account of the differences in cultures of negotiators.[2] In the Bougainville situation, however, culture (in combination

1. Notable exceptions include work by Kevin Avruch, for example, *Culture and Conflict Resolution* (Washington D.C.: USIP Press, 1998) and Michelle LeBaron, for example, "Transforming Cultural Conflict in an Age of Complexity," in *Berghof Handbook for Conflict Transformation* (Berlin: Berghof Research Centre for Constructive Conflict Management, 2001, available at www.//berghof-handbook.net/documents/publications/lebaron_hb.pdf. [accessed March 24, 2010]).

2. There is extensive literature on this aspect of culture published by the U.S. Institute of Peace. See, for example, Raymond Cohen, *Negotiating across Cultures: International Communication in an Interdependent World* (Washington: USIP Press, 1997); Tamara Wittes, ed., *How Israelis and Palestinians Negotiate: A Cross-Cultural Analysis of the Oslo*

with other aspects of context already mentioned) can be seen as an issue of central importance to understanding the dynamics of both the conflict and the peace process.

Concerning culture and conflict, as discussed in chapter 2, the PNG government and Bougainville Copper Ltd misunderstood local culture and this contributed significantly to the origins of the conflict: those authorizing mining leases ignored customary practices with regard to land ownership, and BCL disregarded local cultural traditions in its treatment of Bougainvillean mine workers.

Concerning culture and peacebuilding, the strong emphasis on customary but Christian-influenced reconciliation processes to restore relationships damaged by conflict has been a powerful part of local dynamics for ending conflict and building peace in Bougainville. But there has been limited interest in any more formal and wide-ranging truth and reconciliation processes in relation to extrajudicial killings and other human rights abuses committed during the Bougainville conflict. The fact that societies throughout PNG share similar approaches to reconciliation meant that both sides in the negotiation of the 2001 agreement in part understood the agreement as contributing to reconciliation of a kind that they were accustomed to in their own societies, and so in this sense, shared culture contributed to the success of the peace process.

Violent Conflict and Positive Impacts

Even violent conflict can contribute to positive developments, for example, in the emergence of civil society consensus against the use of violence to resolve conflict.

Those involved in peacebuilding interventions tend to assume that violence and indeed conflict are negative, and that all possible efforts should be made to prevent or limit them. In fact, while tendencies toward violence during a peacebuilding intervention need to be contained, conflict is not only to be expected, but is also a natural part of a peacebuilding process. Further, as the Bougainville case suggests, not all the consequences of violent conflict before or during a peacebuilding

Peace Process (Washington: USIP Press, 2005); Charles Cogan, *French Negotiating Behavior: Dealing with La Grande Nation* (Washington: USIP Press, 2003); Michael Blaker, Paul Giarra, and Ezra Vogel, eds., *Case Studies in Japanese Negotiating Behavior* (Washington: USIP Press, 2005).

intervention are necessarily negative—some may even contribute to peacebuilding.

It seems often forgotten that conflict is inherent in all societies and in any political system; the more important issue is to find ways to limit the extent to which force or violence is applied in the course of conflict. The development of the democratic political systems of western Europe, which are to a considerable extent the models for democratic systems generally, are in large part the result of responses to violent conflict. Indeed, those systems are designed to limit tendencies to resort to use of violence to resolve conflict. It would not be going too far to say that many of the most significant safeguards associated with democratic political systems—including the concept of the rule of law and the recognition of the need for protection of fundamental human rights—have emerged from efforts on the part of peoples to impose limits on the use of violence by the state and by groups in society.

With its remarkable cultural and linguistic diversity and brief period of very limited impact by colonial regimes, preconflict Bougainville presented a weak basis for nation building and state building and the growth of acceptance of the rule of law. While nine years of violent conflict from 1988 to 1997 had terrible impacts, at the same time that period contributed to a strong community consciousness of the damage caused by the conflict. In effect, the experience of conflict and violence seems to have contributed to significant internally generated limitations on the use of violence—a broad societal consensus that violence is no longer an acceptable means of resolving conflict, especially, but not only, between communities. That is not to say that violence no longer occurs in Bougainville—the deaths in local conflicts in south Bougainville between 2005 and 2009 attest to the fact that it does (though in fact levels of violence in Bougainville now are much less than in many other parts of PNG). But when violence does occur, a wide range of pressures tends to emerge from within communities to stop it and to prevent such violence from recurring. Such pressures are not always successful—as the long period of localized violence (late 2005–09) illustrates. But ample evidence also demonstrates that despite initial failed efforts to end violence, communities have continued to press for reconciliation and, in the long run, their efforts often bear fruit.

The same concerns about the need to minimize violence have contributed to widely held views about the need for the state—especially the police—to avoid the use of violence in its dealings with communities. This concern underlies provisions of the 2004 Constitution for the Autonomous Region of Bougainville that provide for a police service rather than a "police force" (as is the case with the PNG constitution). The latter term was rejected quite explicitly. The Bougainville Constitution (section 148) calls for the Bougainville police service to "develop rehabilitatory and reconciliatory concepts of policing," to "work in harmony with communities and encourage community participation in its activities," and to "support and work with traditional chiefs . . . to resolve disputes and maintain law and order in communities." Such concepts largely reflect the rejection of the policing model previously experienced in Bougainville, one seen as having contributed to the use of considerable violence against Bougainvilleans by police mobile squads in the first months of the conflict (1988–89). This violence was a major factor in the escalation of the conflict at a time when otherwise it might well have been manageable.

To the extent that civil society is regarded as the combination of individuals into groups separate from the state that together develop common norms that become accepted as limits on the actions of the state and groups in society, then the beginnings of an emerging civil society may be evident in Bougainville.[3] This is not occurring as a result of the measures most commonly pursued by international interventions seeking to promote civil society (donor funding allocated to support development of local NGOs), but rather through broad-based societal responses to the experience of terrible conflict, responses that cut across cultural and linguistic divisions. In view of the uncertainty of the situation highlighted by ongoing divisions and local conflict in Bougainville, however, it is too early to draw definitive conclusions about the extent and sustainability of this development.

3. There are, of course, other perspectives on the nature of civil society.

Opportunities and Ambiguities in Promoting Women's Involvement in Peacebuilding

Opportunities to pursue the widely accepted goal of international interventions promoting increased involvement of women in peacebuilding can be limited by cultural and other contextual factors.

There is a growing international consensus on the importance not only of women's roles in conflict resolution and peacebuilding but also of their involvement in international peacebuilding interventions, in part both reflected by and responding to UN Security Council Resolution 1325. On the face of it, Bougainville would seem an ideal case for such an approach, because the traditional status of women in most Bougainvillean societies is relatively high and their traditional roles extended to conflict resolution. In fact, as the peace process developed, cultural and other contextual factors came to the fore, limiting the opportunities for participation by women. As a result, there was limited scope for the international intervention to influence the situation.

As already discussed, a major factor contributing to the lack of involvement by women in the negotiations for the 2001 agreement was that many in the almost exclusively male leadership of the factions felt that with the end of the conflict, it was time for women to return to their customary roles, leaving men to occupy the public political space. Hence, the marginalization of women reflected the realities of the patriarchal side of Bougainville society.

On the other hand, both the conflict and the peace process have allowed some Bougainville women the opportunity to undertake new and more public roles, such as leading local reconciliation efforts, participating in NGO activities, organizing marches and other public activities in support of peace, and participating in early stages of the peace talks. While women were little involved in the negotiation of the 2001 peace agreement, it was generally accepted that women should be involved in the constitution-making process in Bougainville from 2002 to 2004. Their participation contributed to the constitution reserving three of the 40 elected seats in the legislature for the ABG for women. No such arrangements had existed in the preconflict Bougainville provincial government or the PNG national legislature. This development arguably reflects changing perceptions about the significance of women's roles in

Bougainville and is partially a reflection of the role that some women had played during the peace process.

Dealing with a Conflict Involving Loose Coalitions Rather than Defined Parties

The second category of lessons concerns the ways in which those involved in development and management of the Bougainville peace process, inclusive of the international intervention, dealt with some of the practical difficulties arising from the nature of the parties to the process. Rather than being clearly defined, the groups involved in the peace process were loose and shifting coalitions. Originally they included the two main Bougainvillean coalitions supporting the process, themselves always loose alliances. At various points, these coalitions divided, as when Ona separated from the BRA/BIG leadership, and the dissident pro-integrationist leaders refused to work with the BPC during much of 1999. The PNG government was itself a coalition of parts of government that often had difficulty cooperating. In 1998 the elements loosely associated with Ona also formed their own group of those who refused to support the process—the Me'ekamui government, in association with the MDF. In 2003 they were joined for a period by Musingku, who, since the death of Ona, claimed to have inherited Ona's authority, contrary to the claims of two other groups, namely the MGU and the original Me'ekamui government, and all three are supported by their own MDF or other armed elements. Although the Me'ekamui leaders opposed the peace process for the 10 years since 1997, that situation has since changed, with first the MGU leaders tentatively entering a partnership with the ABG under the Panguna Communiqué in August 2007, and then the original Me'ekamui government beginning to engage with the ABG in March 2010. But even then, some MDF elements have remained outside, as has Musingku. This case study has presented approaches to this complexity taken by Bougainvillean leaders who have supported the peace process. These have chiefly been guided by a commitment to finding ways to move forward without conflict and have not been carefully planned or managed. The few simple scenarios outlined do not involve any remarkable lessons, but rather some details of what was learned to manage the complexity. And these might have some relevance beyond the particular context of the Bougainville situation.

Patience—Allowing Time for Workable Coalitions to Emerge

In a situation involving loose coalitions, a successful peace process is likely to be long and unpredictable, so patience is needed as different groupings emerge, change, and (sometimes) fade.

It will be difficult for those involved in an international intervention to immediately understand the factors involved in how loose coalitions form, change, and break up. In the Bougainville case, it was vital that such actors were patient and that the organizations involved in the intervention were prepared to be involved for the extended period necessary for workable coalitions to emerge. In the period since the PMG and the UNOMB departed Bougainville, that same patience has been needed by the Bougainville leaders committed to the peace process as they have dealt with the several groups associated with Ona as well as other groups involved in the complex localized conflict in south Bougainville.

Peace Initiatives That Don't End a Violent Conflict Have Not Necessarily Failed

In a complex conflict involving loose coalitions, it may be especially difficult to achieve a lasting resolution without numerous efforts to engage, and even if many of these do not end the conflict, they may still provide the foundations for the ultimately successful process.

It was extremely difficult to achieve a lasting solution in the various interactions between the opposing groups in the Bougainville conflict, not just because of the hostility and suspicion with which they regarded one another, but also because it was difficult to find a common position among the loose coalitions that opposed one another. On the other hand, the many peace initiatives that were so often criticized as failures in the period from 1989 to 1997, in fact, contributed a great deal to the ultimate success of the process regarded as beginning in New Zealand in mid-1997.

Among other things, the early initiatives encouraged the emergence of a moderate leadership; provided vital experience for—and links among—Bougainville and PNG negotiators and key Australian, New Zealand, and UN figures; built an understanding of the complex Bougainville context among international community actors; permitted exploration of options by leaders on all sides; and excluded approaches that did not work.

The same kind of learning and experience has since been gained by the Bougainville leadership from what appeared initially to have been unsuccessful efforts to engage the Me'ekamui leadership in the peace process.

Engaging with All Groups

Where loose coalitions are operating, those encouraging development of a peace process or managing an intervention in support of a process must be ready to engage with all groups.

Through most of the 1990s, the Australian government refused to engage with representatives of the BRA and the BIG, whereas New Zealand maintained communication with their representatives. Those lines of communication were critical to the organizing of the first peace talks in mid-1997. Similarly in the first years of the peace process, as groups split and reformed, communication with all was essential. Even since 2005, as the confused situation with the Me'ekamui government, the MDF, and Noah Musingku has developed in unexpected ways, the ABG has been unable to communicate directly with these various groups and tension and conflict has been most likely to occur. When there has been engagement, the situation has generally been more manageable.

Engagement and communication with groups apparently unwilling to engage has always been essential to finding ways of encouraging or facilitating such groups to join the peace process. Engaging such groups has often taken considerable time and effort and has at times seemed unproductive. That was the initial experience in the mid-1990s when "moderate" Bougainville leadership made efforts to engage with the BIG and BRA leaders, and it has continued to be the experience of efforts to engage with the Me'ekamui and MDF leaders in the period since the UN mission left Bougainville (2005). Over time, willingness and efforts to engage have contributed to the emergence of trust and relationships, and opportunities for previously dissident groups to participate in the peace process have been found, often quite unexpectedly.

The Australian Department of Foreign Affairs and Trade has barred AusAID personnel from entering the "no-go-zone" through the Morgan Junction roadblock since the signing of the Panguna Communiqué in August 2007, this indicates the importance of engaging with all groups. Similarly, by refusing to engage with the BIG and BRA leadership in the 1990s, Australia was stymied in some of its peacebuilding efforts. Yet the evidence from 1997 was that much was clearly gained by broader efforts to engage with all possible groups. It is unclear why the apparent lesson from the earlier stages of the peace process has no longer been applied by Australia since 2007.

Look for Opportunities to Support Moderate Leaders and Moderate Coalitions

Where opposing groupings are loose, and ongoing conflict is having widespread negative impacts, moderate leadership can emerge unexpectedly, offering opportunities for opponents to engage and perhaps to develop new coalitions, and peacebuilders need to be ready to support such leaders and coalitions.

With all the opposing groups in Bougainville suffering from the impacts of the conflict in 1996–97, there was room for moderate leadership to come to the fore. Opposing groups could then engage in ways that had not previously been possible. In the process, a new coalition of moderate Bougainvillean leadership emerged that negotiated the peace agreement on behalf of Bougainville. Although the moderate coalition faced opposition from both dissenting pro-secessionists and pro-integrationists, it proved robust, in large part because the international intervention was put in place quickly (the TMG was in situ within weeks of the Burnham Truce) and provided security and support for the emerging coalition.

Inclusive Negotiation Teams and Consultation Systems Help Maintain Coalitions

Loose coalitions usually comprise multiple elements, and when such a coalition is contributing to peacebuilding, all elements need to feel part of the process, and large and inclusive negotiating teams as well as good arrangements for consulting constituencies before and after negotiations can help to ensure no element feels excluded, thereby contributing to maintaining the coalition.

In the Bougainville case, where even the opposing combatant groups were loosely allied groups that could be in conflict with one another at the local level, the moderate coalition formed around the BPC in 1999 could only be maintained by ensuring that there was constant inclusion of all possible elements of not only the BRA and BRF, but also other groups (BIG, BTG, the pro-integration leadership, and others). This outcome was achieved mainly through very large Bougainville delegations to most negotiations, inclusive of large teams handling the negotiation of the 2001 peace agreement and by encouraging representatives of the main groups to constantly consult their membership, in advance and after as many negotiating sessions as possible.

Encouraging and Supporting Local Processes

The third category of lessons relates to the importance of those leading the Bougainville intervention understanding and supporting the local peace process. The existence of a strong locally initiated and controlled peace process, and the fact that the intervention was largely undertaken to support that process, had benefits for both the local actors and those managing the intervention. There were also some significant aspects of the way the local process operated that may be of particular interest to those involved in peacebuilding interventions elsewhere.

Local Ownership and Conflict Resolution through the Unfolding of Local Dynamics

The more a peace process is initiated and controlled by local actors rather than the international intervention supporting it, the more the scope both for local ownership of the process and the resolution of inevitable tensions and conflicts through unfolding local dynamics.

Because the international intervention in Bougainville was playing a mainly facilitative and supportive role, with Bougainvillean groups and the PNG government clearly setting the agenda and determining the shape and direction of the peace process, there was usually pressure on the often divided Bougainvillean groups and PNG to engage directly with each other to find accommodations. The international community supplied the secure environment within which such processes could develop. At times it encouraged particular developments, prodding here or mediating there, but at no time did it seek to dominate or control. In such a situation, the local parties felt ownership of and commitment to the process.

As is so often the case in complex postconflict situations, access to power under new political arrangements was at stake at various points in the peace process. In large part as a result, tensions and splits occurred among local actors, at various points causing significant problems for the process. However, because the parties were committed to the process and to managing so as to achieve positive outcomes, their leadership came under locally generated pressure to deal with tensions and differences that threatened the process. By contrast, if the international community had played a dominant role, the parties would have been far less likely to take responsibility for dealing with such problems.

More generally, if the parties to a conflict do not have direct roles in the management of the peace process, then the process and its outcomes are more likely to be manipulated by the international community (for example to achieve its own exit goals). Alternatively, the international community is more likely to be subject to efforts by local actors to manipulate the process to the advantage of particular local interests.

Legitimacy and Sustainability of the International Intervention

Supporting a locally initiated and controlled peace process should encourage local consent for an intervention, improving its legitimacy in the eyes of local actors and contributing to its sustainability.

The legitimacy of peacekeepers and other international actors in conflict resolution and peacebuilding processes relies on local consent. When peacekeepers and others play roles that are clearly subordinate to, and determined by, local actors, they will almost inevitably be seen in a different and more positive light than if their presence has been imposed in one way or another. (It is recognized, of course, that there may be situations in which it is not possible to get the kind of consent and cooperation that the international community received in Bougainville.)[4]

4. For a more detailed discussion of issues of legitimacy and sustainability of the international intervention in Bougainville, see Regan, "The Bougainville Intervention."

Contribution of the Constitution-Making Process to the Peace Process

Constitution-making processes, and not just the contents of postconflict constitutions, can make significant contributions to peacebuilding.

Postconflict constitutional change and development tend to occur in at least two distinct situations. The first involves situations where struggles for control of the state have been an important aspect of the conflict. In such cases either major revisions to, or complete replacement of, the existing national constitution can often occur as part of the resolution of the conflict (for example, to provide redress of discriminatory or exclusionary arrangements that contributed to conflict). The second involves situations where the conflict has involved efforts by a minority to secede from the state. In such cases, postconflict constitutional change can often take two distinct forms, neither of which is mutually exclusive. One involves changes to the national constitution to accommodate the secessionists, such as through autonomy or power-sharing arrangements. The other involves empowering the making of a subnational constitution providing structures and processes of government of the autonomous area.

In general, the focus of the international community in relation to postconflict constitution making tends to be on contents of such constitutional changes rather than on the processes that produce them. Contents can, of course, be vitally important, for example, by reducing sources of conflict through such items as provisions on discrimination against minorities, democratization, power sharing, autonomy arrangements, increased political opportunities for women and other marginalized groups, and so on. But constitution-making processes can also make significant contributions to peacebuilding, for example, by

- supporting conflict resolution and reconciliation by providing a framework within which a wide range of interest groups can consult, negotiate, and develop consensus on ways to address root causes of conflict and future steps;
- influencing the contents of a postconflict constitution to meet local needs, including addressing factors that contribute to conflict and ensuring that concerns and rights of minorities are addressed; and

- ensuring that citizens (including former combatants and other actors in the conflict) understand and are committed to the postconflict constitution.

However, where conflict-resolution and peacebuilding processes are dominated by the international community, the timetables, agendas, and even the lack of experience of international organizations in constitution making can all conspire to greatly restrict the possible benefits that can emerge from constitution-making processes.[5]

Constitutional arrangements developed through the Bougainville peace process had two distinct dimensions—first, the amendments at the national level to implement the 2001 Bougainville Peace Agreement and, second, the Constitution for the Autonomous Region of Bougainville. Each set of arrangements was developed through separate processes, each taking more than two years—the former from mid-1999 to early 2002, the latter from 2002 to 2004—the kind of extended timetables with which managers of international interventions are usually not comfortable. In both cases, locally controlled processes delivered innovative approaches that local actors believed met local needs. At the same time, local control of the processes led to the rejection of some possible elements of postconflict constitutional arrangements that many in the international community tend to see as standard, such as power sharing and a transitional justice process.

Recognition of Local Capacity to Develop Original Solutions to Difficult Problems

The capacity of local actors to find their own solutions to the difficult problems that they face should be recognized by any international intervention.

In the process of the unfolding of local dynamics in a peace process, constructive and in many cases original solutions to difficult problems can be found—something less likely if the international community is

5. For a discussion of aspects of such situations, see Michele Brandt, "Constitutional Assistance in Post-Conflict Countries: Cambodia, East Timor and Afghanistan" (New York: UNDP, 2005), and Anthony J. Regan, "Constitution-Making in East Timor: Missed Opportunities?" in Dionisio Soares, Michael Maley, James J. Fox, and Anthony J. Regan, eds., *Elections and Constitution Making in East Timor* (Canberra: State, Society and Governance in Melanesia Project, Australian National University, 2003), 35–42.

in control or dominant. In general, it could be expected that local solutions may better take account of context than solutions developed and perhaps imposed by the intervention. Local solutions can apply to both matters of design of the peace process and matters of substance of the political arrangements included in the peace agreement. A few examples will suffice to make the point.

In particular, the proposal that the TMG (and the PMG) should be unarmed was in many ways one of genius, remarkably well suited to the circumstances in the Bougainville case. An example involving substance of political arrangements concerns the combination of autonomy and referendum as a response to demands for independence, together with the constitutional protection of these arrangements through "double entrenchment." Already, aspects of these arrangements have been examined as possible precedents by separatist rebels engaging in peace processes in South Sudan, Mindanao, Aceh, Sri Lanka, and Nagaland (Northeast India).

An example involving a combination of process and substance concerns the creative arrangements in the Bougainville Peace Agreement for sequencing and providing linkages between steps in the agreed disarmament process and the obligation of PNG to amend its constitution to provide for the agreed arrangements. The parties to the Bougainville process thereby dealt effectively with issues that have caused problems in many other peace processes, namely disarmament of local militias, withdrawal of PNG security forces, and implementation of newly agreed political arrangements. In essence, each side agreed to implement a step that was to some degree against its interests, provided that the other side did the same. Steps by one became a precondition for steps by the other. Verification by the international intervention that agreed-upon steps in relation to disarmament had in fact been taken was also essential.

Similar links between "decommissioning" of weapons and constitutional or electoral steps could perhaps have been helpful in the Northern Ireland peace process. But such linkage and sequencing arrangements could also be adapted to meet quite distinct goals. They might be applied, for example, in a situation where a national government is concerned about risks that a new autonomous regime proposed as part of a peace settlement may be at risk of either being dominated by, say, an antidemocratic group or one that ignores human rights norms. In such circumstances the national government could negotiate for specific, verifiable benchmarks to measure the implementation of democratization or for human rights protections that, once achieved, would "trigger" further steps that the autonomous regime sees as vital to its interests. Such arrangements might usefully have been considered in other recent conflict situations, such as Nepal or even Sri Lanka.

Importance of Precedents

While there is no template for use in any given peacebuilding intervention, knowledge of what has worked well or has caused problems elsewhere can be useful, both for the international community and for local actors.

Consideration of the need for understanding context underlines the need for great care when considering possible models and templates for international peacebuilding interventions. While much can be gained by applying appropriate lessons from experience elsewhere and precedents of various kinds can be useful, it is normally essential to adapt existing models and templates to the given conflict and its unique context.

On the other hand, access to information about precedents is important to the international community and to local actors as well. The international community is often concerned, in particular, as to how other interventions have been conducted. (In cases where it exerts more control than was the case in Bougainville, the international community can also be interested in precedents beyond the conduct of the intervention, extending to management of negotiations, conduct of constitution-making processes, and so on, as has been the case, for example, with UN-initiated interventions in such places as Namibia, Cambodia, and Timor Leste.)

There can also be considerable interest in precedents on the part of parties to a peace process. For example, while much in the Bougainville Peace Agreement is unique, the parties made considerable use of international precedents. On the Bougainville side, the proposal for a constitutionally guaranteed but deferred referendum on independence drew on the Noumea Accord of 1998, under which France and Kanak separatists in New Caledonia (in the southwest Pacific—see Map 1) had agreed on similar arrangements. Proposals for foreign affairs–type powers for Bougainville drew on, among others, the autonomy arrangements for Hong Kong under the Basic Law for the Hong Kong Special Administrative Region of the People's Republic of China. Proposals for Bougainville's role in the process for amending the PNG constitutional arrangements implementing the peace agreement drew on provisions of a number of postconflict constitutions (including provisions on subnational government in the Uganda Constitution of 1995). It was important too that reference to such precedents appeared to increase the credibility of such Bougainville proposals in the eyes of PNG government negotiators.

In fact, an important role for the international community in many conflict resolution and peacebuilding processes may not be so much to introduce what it might see as appropriate templates for postconflict state building and constitution making, but rather to make available to local actors information about potentially relevant precedents that such actors might not readily be able to learn of otherwise. In this way, the capacity of local actors to negotiate on the basis of informed choices that meet local needs can be much enhanced.

Aspects of Organizing and Managing the International Intervention

The fourth category of lessons concerns aspects of how the design and management of the international intervention in Bougainville supported the local peace process and achieved a "light footprint."

Designed and Managed to Support the Local Peace Process

If possible the main role of an international intervention should involve support for the local peace process, and the intervention should be designed and managed accordingly.

It follows from what has been discussed about the importance of local ownership that, where possible, international peacebuilding interventions should be designed and managed with a primary emphasis on the role of supporting the local peace process. There can be tendencies for international actors involved in a peacebuilding intervention to see a mainly supportive role as unduly restrictive, leading to pressure to play what might be seen as more significant roles. This tendency was sometimes evident in the Bougainville case, probably flowing from the limited understanding that some personnel in the PMG, in particular, had of the situation in Bougainville, and from the frustration that some from the international community felt at what they saw as their relatively limited role. For example, some wanted more active roles in mediation and negotiation about issues dividing the parties, while others envisaged more of an active developmental role for the PMG. In general, however, such undoubted pressures toward "mission creep" were kept under control, and the focus on simply "being there" in a supportive role was maintained.

Sensitive and Creative Leadership and Management Required

An international intervention in support of a local peace process requires sensitive and creative leadership and management, with specialized knowledge of the local context.

Although limiting the role of the international intervention to supporting the local process may seem restrictive, in fact, leadership and management must be particularly sensitive and creative if such a role is to be carried out effectively. It requires understanding the context and an ability to be sensitive to changes and developments in the situation that may require response from the intervention.

In relation to understanding context, in the Bougainville case the extended tours of duty undertaken by the successive directors of the UN mission contributed to their having a good understanding of the context. By contrast, the limited local knowledge of TMG and PMG military commanders was compensated through use of both experienced senior civil servants from New Zealand and Australia with knowledge of Bougainville as the deputy leaders of the TMG and PMG. The sharing of leadership responsibility between military and civilian personnel seems to have been a useful way of encouraging sensitive and creative leadership. The practice of having a senior civilian working alongside a military commander of overseas operations in complex conflict or postconflict situations is now common practice for Australia. It has been part of deployments in East Timor, Solomon Islands, Afghanistan, and

Iraq. It was the experience of the TMG and the PMG in Bougainville that established the precedent for such arrangements.[6]

Personnel with Specialist Local Knowledge

If an international intervention is to understand context and operate effectively in support of a local peace process, it should draw on personnel with specialized knowledge of the local situation.

Because understanding context is of such critical importance, any international peacebuilding intervention needs a strong capacity in that regard available from the earliest stages of planning the intervention and throughout its operation. This will usually mean relying heavily on people with local knowledge, including academics and practitioners and a range of local actors. Equipped with local knowledge, the ability of those planning and managing an intervention to both understand the context in which the intervention occurs and to work constructively with local actors will grow.

Working with All Parties

To be effective an international intervention usually needs to be perceived by local actors as neutral, and to do that it must be seen to be open to working with all parties.

Those involved in interventions sometimes make judgments about which parties or factions it is possible to work with. They may even encourage such parties to reach consensus on excluding other parties or factions regarded as difficult or expected to be a negative influence on the process. There are obvious risks in such approaches, not least that of being seen to be partisan, something that will almost always undermine the effectiveness of an intervention.

In the Bougainville case, once the intervention was in place, the combination of Australian government sensitivity to the suspicion with which Australia was regarded in Bougainville and PNG, and the extent to which the local parties were in control of the process, meant that there was little scope for the leaders of the intervention to make judgments about what local actors they would deal with. As a result they were seen as open to dealing with all. This was a significant factor in the

6. I am grateful to David Hallett for informing me of this fact.

neutrality of the intervention being widely accepted, despite the initial strong suspicion of Australian leadership by Bougainville elements.

But No Intervention Is Completely Neutral

While an intervention must aim to be neutral, it needs to be recognized that it is not possible for such an activity to be completely neutral in its impacts.

Whatever the good intentions and best efforts of the designers and managers, no intervention can be completely neutral in its impacts. By its presence alone, the intervention has uneven impacts on the parties to a peace process, factions within the parties, and leaders of parties and factions, as well as other groups. There will almost always be some opportunities for local leaders to exploit advantages that they derive from the intervention, or to otherwise manipulate the interventions, often without the leaders of the intervention being able to understand what is happening. Further, despite best efforts to behave neutrally, in a highly sensitive postconflict situation it can be easy for the actions of an intervention to be interpreted as partisan. With a good understanding of context, such impacts can sometimes be reduced, but seldom completely eliminated.

In the Bougainville case, although those managing the intervention made considerable efforts to ensure they were perceived as neutral, there were various problems that can be illustrated by a few examples. Well-intended allocation of funding in support of local initiatives associated with the peace process in various cases was seen as favoring particular faction leaders, contributing to local tensions. Officials of the PNG government at times suspected bias on the part of the UN mission and the PMG, mainly because the BRA and other Bougainville groups were treated as parties of equal status to PNG during the often tense process for negotiating the 2001 Bougainville Peace Agreement. While Francis Ona and his followers chose to exclude themselves from the peace process, they nevertheless resented what they saw as the benefits that other groups obtained from associating with the intervention, probably a factor in some incidents involving theft of UN and UNDP vehicles by MDF elements.

One of the actions of the intervention that probably helped to improve perceptions of neutrality was the AusAID funding to provide key independent advisers to all of the parties involved in the negotiation for the

Bougainville Peace Agreement. This was not a planned step on the part of the leaders of the intervention or of AusAID, but rather a response to specific requests for support from each party for assistance to engage particular advisers with whom they already had established links.

Dividing Responsibilities between Parts of an International Intervention

There can be advantages in involving a number of actors from the international community in peacebuilding interventions and in spreading responsibility for distinct aspects of the intervention among them.

In the Bougainville case, several benefits resulted from the cooperative involvement of distinct entities (the UN mission, a regional coalition, and donor agencies) handling relatively distinct sets of responsibilities in a broad-based international community intervention. First, despite strong suspicion of Australia in Bougainville, Australian involvement in the process was important for financial and other reasons. In such circumstances, the initial leadership provided by New Zealand and the involvement of other countries from the region made Australian involvement in the process more acceptable and provided time for perceptions to change. Only after the process was well established did the lead shift to Australia. Second, UN involvement was particularly important to the BRA and BIG, largely because of their suspicion of Australia. It also acted as a counter to any fears that Australia, as the dominant regional power, would have undue influence over New Zealand. The UN role of monitoring the TMG and the PMG also increased the acceptability of the UN mission to a PNG government that had concerns about even the regional intervention undermining its sovereignty.

Third, dividing roles among the key international parties also had practical advantages. For example, the TMG and the PMG had responsibility for monitoring the truce and ceasefire, respectively, while the UN mission played more general monitoring, chairing, and mediating roles. Had the UN been required to monitor the truce and ceasefire as well, inclusive of investigation of violations, perceptions of its neutrality could readily have been undermined, thereby compromising its ability to act as a mediator, as chair of the main negotiating and consultative processes, and as supervisor of the weapons disposal process.

In summary, the Bougainville experience suggests that the possible advantages of a broad-based international intervention in conflict resolution and peacebuilding processes include

- providing a basis for the involvement of a major international actor in those instances when local actors oppose or are otherwise sensitive about its being involved on its own or taking a dominant role in the process, and yet where there might be strong geopolitical concerns or issues about the resource needs of the intervention that make its involvement desirable;
- enabling sensitive responsibilities to be divided among various international actors, which, if vested in the same entity, could undermine capacity to carry out other responsibilities; and
- increasing the likelihood that the whole intervention is seen as something greater than the sum of its constituent elements, so that if problems occur with one or another of them in the eyes of a local actor, the credibility of the overall intervention does not suffer greatly in the eyes of the local community.

Cooperation between Military and Civilian Components of Those Planning for and Implementing an Intervention

In addition to dividing responsibilities among parts of an intervention, there can be advantages in sharing responsibilities between civilian and military leadership in the process of planning and implementing the peace monitoring or peacekeeping part of an intervention.

In the Bougainville situation, there were advantages in the "intense cooperation" between military and civilian agencies involved in both the planning for and the implementation of the TMG and the PMG.[7] Inevitably military personnel took the leadership roles of what were largely groups of specialist military personnel. But there would have been grave difficulties for military leaders who had little prior experience of Bougainville, PNG, or Melanesia to either plan or implement the operations without extensive input from experienced and senior civilian officials.

7. Mortlock, "Lessons from Bougainville," 471.

Unarmed Personnel and Causal Mechanisms of Peacekeeping

The efficacy of peacekeepers in fragile postconflict situations involving distrustful belligerents can sometimes be enhanced if the peacekeepers are unarmed.

Deployment of unarmed peacekeepers (in Bougainville, called "monitors") offers perspectives on the causal mechanisms by which peacekeepers keep the peace in fragile postconflict situations. While the belligerents in such situations may enter a peace process because they are losing faith in the efficacy of armed conflict for achieving their goals, they usually tend to remain deeply distrustful of one another. In the Bougainville case, the unarmed peacekeepers provided local mediation when minor ceasefire violations occurred or when actions by one side or the other could readily have been misinterpreted by opposing forces, thereby preventing escalation of such incidents into renewed conflict.

But in addition to these more normal aspects of peacekeeping, there was some moral pressure flowing from the fact that most members of the TMG and the PMG were soldiers, all of whom were unarmed. The request for the TMG and the PMG to be unarmed was originally made by the Bougainville parties, largely because they feared that the presence of armed regional forces could readily be misinterpreted by Ona and his supporters, thereby increasing the risk of violent clashes. In doing so, the Bougainville parties took on the obligation of ensuring the security of TMG and PMG members, thereby taking a high degree of ownership of the process. Further, it soon became clear that there was a powerful symbolism and even something of an unspoken challenge for the armed belligerents in the presence of uniformed warriors without their guns, a challenge probably enhanced by the inclusion of female members in the monitoring teams.[8]

A "Light Footprint" Combined with Greater Flexibility?

The pressure for an early exit that is likely to accompany a "light footprint" international intervention may sometimes need to be tempered with attention to a need for enough flexibility to provide additional support if there are risks of conflict being renewed.

---

8. For more on the origins and experience of the TMG and the PMG, see Wehner and Denoon, eds., *Without a Gun.*

Although the localized armed conflict that developed in the south of Bougainville in late 2005 could not have readily been anticipated, the difficulties of the Bougainville situation are such that flexible arrangements were warranted for the international intervention, including allowing for a small regional "force" that could have assisted the ABG with renewed weapons disposal efforts.

Problems in Managing Impacts of Funding and the State Building Aspects of an Intervention

The fifth category of lessons involves the recognition of the complexities and difficulties for an international intervention in both understanding the impacts of funding of local peacebuilding activities and managing state-building efforts.

Unintended Negative Consequences of International Funding

Financial contributions intended to support peacebuilding can have unintended and negative impacts, especially when the local context is not thoroughly understood.

No calculation has been made of the costs incurred by the international community's support for the Bougainville peace process. In addition to the not insignificant costs of the TMG, the PMG, the Bougainville Transitional Team (BTT), and the UN mission, there have been other international financial contributions, either to the peace process or to humanitarian assistance, reconstruction, and development in Bougainville. While much of that support has been designed with care and creativity (for example, the AusAID-funded project for upgrading and maintaining the main trunk road), other aspects of funding have undermined patterns of self-reliance and contributed to tensions and conflict. As discussed elsewhere in this monograph, they have included funding for small projects described as "peace dividends," payments of allowances to people to take part in negotiations and other peace process activities, payments to facilitate reconciliations, and incentive payments made in relation to weapons disposal.

"Now Comes the Hard Part": Inherent Difficulties in State Building

The state-building and economic reconstruction activities of a peacebuilding intervention can be extremely difficult to manage and should not ignore international development assistance experience, which can illuminate difficulties and possible approaches.

On the basis that peacebuilding processes need to tackle the root causes of conflict (so as to reduce the likelihood of renewed conflict), the commonly accepted template for peacebuilding tends to include state building and economic reconstruction. While extensive international community involvement in state-building efforts as part of peacebuilding interventions is a relatively new phenomenon, other parts of the international community—mainly development assistance agencies—have had extensive involvement in a great many international state-building, capacity-building, and economic development initiatives over the past 50 years. In doing so, they have met with limited success, more perhaps having been learned about what does not work than what does.[9]

Little of that hard-earned experience seems to be influencing the state-building and economic reconstruction efforts being undertaken as part of peacebuilding processes. This seems to be as much the case in Iraq and Afghanistan as in the Australian-led Regional Assistance Mission to the Solomon Islands (or Australia's capacity-building programs for PNG in the period since 2004—the Enhanced Cooperation Program and the Strongim Gavman Program, both intended to assist a so-called weak or fragile state and to reduce the danger of that state's becoming a failed state). A significant part of the reason for this failure to consider the relevance of considerable existing experience relates to one simple fact: peacebuilding exercises are driven by presidents and prime ministers and secretaries of state and ministers for foreign affairs, rather than by secretaries and ministers responsible for international development assistance or the heads of unilateral development agencies.

One particular lesson from development assistance that should be carefully considered in peacebuilding interventions relates to the dif-

9. See, for example, Peter Morgan, "Technical Assistance: Correcting the Precedents," *Development Policy Journal*, vol. 2 (December 2002): 1–22.

ficulties involved in strengthening failed, weak, or fragile states through capacity-building efforts driven by donors. Two points made by Francis Fukuyama in his 2004 analysis of international state-building experience are relevant hnotNOere.[10] First, in general, sustainable public sector reform does not occur unless there is a domestic demand for it. In other words, there will normally be little chance of sustainable reform directed at building state capacity in postconflict situations unless the local population is committed to and taking a leading role in the design and implementation of reform. Second, not only does the international community have little understanding of how to undertake successful capacity building where state capacity is weak, but where such capacity building is attempted, it usually results in the "sucking out" of local capacity. A key reason for the latter phenomenon is that the specialist staff that the international community supplies to undertake capacity-building work also tends to come under pressure to ensure that the organization that they work with actually achieves results. In consequence, they tend to undertake active roles that undermine local capacity, often resulting in frustrated officers becoming uncooperative or even leaving the civil service.

In the Bougainville situation, state building was not a focus of the TMG, the PMG, or the UN mission, although it was (in brief) for the BTT. For the most part, state building has been left to development assistance specialists, in particular, AusAID, New Zealand Aid, and (to a lesser extent) the UNDP. In general, these agencies have proceeded carefully. There has been some capacity-building support to the police, but until about 2009 little was provided to the Bougainville administration beyond limited and mainly part-time technical assistance, as requested by the administration, and installation of the Governance and Implementation Fund, intended to provide some incentives for improved budgeting and financial management.[11] While the administration struggled

10. Francis Fukuyama, *State-Building: Governance and World Order in the 21st Century* (Ithaca: Cornell University Press, 2004), 39–42.

11. The situation with the PNG police working in Bougainville is different. New Zealand has provided technical support and capacity building for some years, and AusAID has been providing capacity building support since 2007. However, while some

to perform, there were some gradual improvements, driven in part by increasing local pressure on the ABG for better performance. Although the situation was far from impressive, it seems likely that locally controlled reform efforts were more sustainable than major outside interventions would have been. From early 2009 the situation has changed, with AusAID providing (at the Bougainville administration's request) eight full-time, capacity-building advisers. It would be an interesting case study to examine the impact of this new form of support.

In general, much more needs to be done by the international community to build a better understanding of alternative state-building strategies that may be more effective in the context of peacebuilding interventions. Although limited in scope, the state-building aspect of the international intervention in Bougainville is ongoing and has so far been far less impressive and effective than other aspects of the intervention.

functions and powers in relation to the police have been delegated to Bougainville, in practice the extent of ABG control of the police is quite limited.

Conclusion

Reconsidering the "Light Footprint" of the Bougainville Intervention

As discussed in the introduction to this monograph, the extensive agenda of activities that increasingly tends to be assumed as necessary to an international intervention seems to be influencing a tendency toward an increased "weight" in the "footprint" of interventions. Yet Bougainville is a case where the footprint remained relatively light, despite the same extensive agenda of activities being adopted by the international intervention. To put it another way, despite the broad scope of its activities, the potential negative impacts of the intervention in terms of excessive domination of the peace process and of local actors were limited. Many of the advantages of this situation are illustrated in the discussion in chapter 7. At the same time, however, it has become evident that there also were perhaps problems inherent in the "light footprint" approach in Bougainville. Without some flexibility to provide further support after the departure of the PMG and the UN, developments from late 2005 put peacebuilding in Bougainville at considerable risk. The key reason was that the "light footprint" came together with pressure for the earliest practicable exit of the only components of the intervention capable of dealing with weapons and armed groups willing to use them. So questions remain as to whether in some ways the intervention was too light, in the sense that significant aspects of the intervention ended too early, or were withdrawn without adequate backup provision being made available.

Hence this brief concluding chapter focuses on just two major questions. The first concerns why a "light footprint" was possible in the particular circumstances of Bougainville. The second concerns whether the footprint was in some ways too light, either in the sense that a critically important part of the intervention (the PMG) departed too early, or in the sense that a capacity should have been maintained after the departure of the PMG that could have supported the parties to the peace process as localized conflict and difficulties with weapons disposal threatened to undermine the process.

Concerning the first question, although there were clear advantages of the "light footprint," there were natural tendencies on the part of some involved in the intervention to take greater control of the process (something evident with some PMG personnel in particular). Why was it that such tendencies were kept under control, with the international community neither seeking to determine the agenda for the peace process nor taking an actively interventionist approach? The many factors that contributed to these outcomes can conveniently be divided into three main groups, all emerging from this study. They are summarized here as accidents of the gradual development of the process, contextual factors, and management and design factors.

Concerning the first of those three, it must be emphasized that unlike many international interventions in the past 10 to 15 years, this was one that was both requested by local actors and evolved gradually, not always with a conscious intent. It was initially expected to be both small scale and to last no more than a few months—New Zealand and Australian civilian and military planners would have been horrified in late 1997 had they known that their personnel would not be leaving Bougainville until the second half of 2003. The expanded timetable and the significant commitments of military and civilian resources required emerged gradually, and always with key planners in Australia and New Zealand reluctant to continue without clear exit strategies. Further, there were always strongly differing opinions in various parts of the Australian and New Zealand governments and bureaucracies, in particular, concerning the appropriate size of the intervention and the extent of the role that it should play, and such arguments tended to result in pressure for moderation in the decisions on such issues. Finally, local actors (particularly but not only in Bougainville) had strong (and in some cases initially opposing) and gradually changing views on the appropriate roles and extent of the international intervention. As a result of such factors and influences, the way the intervention developed was not so much a matter of careful planning, but rather a product of complex interactions of numerous often distinct interests among both international and local actors. In these circumstances, any tendency toward an expansive role for the intervention was unlikely to get free rein.

As for contextual factors contributing to the limited weight of the intervention, one of the most significant was the "mutually hurting stalemate" applicable to all the opposing coalitions of interests by 1997, which in turn contributed to the emergence of moderate leadership in all those groupings. This pushed parties to accept a locally initiated peace process. They were not waiting for international actors to lead the way.

A second set of contextual factors involved the geopolitical situation of Bougainville, with its small diaspora population in an isolated part of a country and with restricted international linkages. Such factors meant that while Bougainville represented a significant security issue in regional terms, there were no significant strategic stakes for any of the actors involved in the international intervention that could reasonably be expected to be damaged by that involvement, other than perhaps Australia's relations with PNG, a factor that only encouraged moderation on the part of Australia, as already discussed. Hence, the geopolitical situation reduced the kinds of pressures that apply to many other international interventions.

A third contextual factor involved wariness on the part of the international community due to the complexity of the Bougainville conflict and awareness of the difficulties of the situation that had emerged through involvement in previous peace initiatives, including the experience of the insertion of the regional peacekeeping force there in October 1994 (as touched on in chapter 3).

A fourth factor involved the wariness of the international intervention on the part of the PNG government and Bougainville parties as a result of their own suspicions of Australia and their prior experience with other international involvement in prior peace initiatives. Another factor involved the desire of the PNG government to protect its sovereignty and to limit the internationalization of a conflict that it regarded as an internal matter.

A final and crucially significant contextual factor involves a major cultural aspect of context, concerning what might be called the culture of reconciliation that is a part of broader Melanesian culture. It provides an orientation and widely understood framework within which people can work toward restoring relationships damaged by conflict. This cultural factor contributed to the parties' having more willingness and capacity to engage with one another than is normally the case in peace processes following long and divisive violent conflict.

In terms of factors involving management and design of the international intervention, a first involves the understanding of the Bougainville context on the part of the key New Zealand and Australian civilian and military officials involved in the early stages of development of the intervention. In particular, the key civilian officials had been closely involved in the Bougainville situation since the late 1980s and so were well aware of the complexities of the situation there. They had already built good personal relationships with many key actors among both the Bougainville factions and the PNG government. As a result, they tended to be open to advice from PNG and Bougainvillean actors, for example, in relation to the TMG and the PMG being unarmed. Second, while parts of the Australian government bureaucracy, in particular, favored a strongly activist and agenda-setting international intervention (notably elements of the military establishment), officers in the Department of Foreign Affairs and Trade with extensive experience of Bougainville, PNG, and the wider Pacific islands took the lead and successfully advocated a less activist approach. Third, the division of responsibilities among those involved in the international intervention helped to ensure moderation in approach, even when particular actors became impatient. For example, in 1997–98 New Zealand took the lead with strong Australian support. In mid-1998 Australia took the lead, but because of the suspicion with which it was regarded, took a tentative approach and always was open to advice from New Zealand, which remained in a strong supportive role. From 1999 the UNPOB director, Ambassador Noel Sinclair, took an increasing leadership role and was an important factor in moderating what on occasion was strong pressure from elements of the Australian bureaucracy to set the agenda and push for a much more rigid timetable for exit of the PMG and completion of the peace process. Fourth, the fact that all elements of the international intervention were unarmed made the TMG and the PMG, in particular, much more sensitive to local concerns than they otherwise might have been; they were careful about maintaining excellent relations with Bougainvillean groups and moderated sometimes strong pressures to set agendas and timetables.

Turning to the second question (as to whether the footprint of the intervention was in fact too light), the first issue arises from matters discussed in chapters 4 and 6. When the PMG's departure was first being planned, late in 2002 and early in 2003, Bougainville parties to the peace process strongly opposed the action, encouraging the Australian government to allow the PMG to remain longer in Bougainville. The Australian authorities, however, were persuaded that the Bougainvillean parties had grown too dependent on the international intervention and needed to be encouraged to find their own solutions and take more responsibility for the whole peace process, without relying on the PMG and the UN mission.

The answer to the question—was the PMG's departure too early?—depends very much on when the question was asked. Because conflict almost never ends completely, but changes in form and intensity, local actors in a peace process may push for continued outside support for extended periods. Because of the emergence of extensive localized conflict in south Bougainville in late 2005 and the difficulties with reconciliation and weapons disposal in the years after the departure of the PMG (in 2003) and the UN mission (in 2005), many Bougainvilleans tended to feel at that time that major components of the intervention had departed Bougainville too early. When considering the same question in early 2010, however, the answer tends to be quite different. Bougainvilleans have gradually developed strategies that so far seem to have been successful in managing the worst of the localized conflict, and some of the major factions previously associated with Francis Ona's leadership are beginning to work with the leaders supporting the peace process. Further, some tentative progress is being made toward development of new weapons disposal programs. On the strength of that evidence, there is support for the assessment made by the Australian authorities in 2002–3 about the need for Bougainvilleans to be less dependent on the international intervention.

The second aspect of the question about whether the footprint was too light concerns whether the international intervention should have provided some form of flexible capacity to Bougainville leaders to deal with localized conflict or disposal of weapons remaining in the hands of groups not part of the 2001–5 disposal process. As discussed in chapter 6, there are arguments in favor of the need for such a capacity. But again, the extent of such a need was far greater in, say, 2006–7 than it appears early in 2010, when some progress in relation to the issues in question seems to be evident. On the other hand, the situation in Bougainville is still unfolding, and it is perhaps too early to provide a definitive answer—to either aspect of the question.

In summary, then, the three groups of factors outlined earlier in this brief chapter were among the most important of many that combined to create strong pressures for a "light footprint" intervention, which, while it suffered from some limitations, in general made an overwhelmingly positive contribution to what must be assessed as a remarkably successful peace process. International peacebuilding interventions very seldom warrant such a broadly positive assessment.

Chronology

Major Events in the Bougainville Conflict and Peace Process

This chronology is intended to assist the reader in understanding the history of Bougainville, as well as the conflict and peace process. More detailed chronologies can be found elsewhere, though at the time of this writing there is no readily available chronology of events in the peace process occurring after about 2002.[1]

30,000 years BP	Buka and Bougainville first populated by human migrants, probably in a series of migrations from the north (through the Bismarck Archipelago).
3,000 years BP	New waves of migration into Buka and Bougainville, again probably from the north.
1767	First recorded European sighting of Buka and Bougainville by Careret, captain of a British vessel.
1768	Bougainville Islands sighted by French expedition under Louis de Bougainville, who names the island.
1884	November: Germany annexes northeast part of New Guinea, including Bismarck Archipelago, leaving eastern boundary of what became known as German New Guinea unclear, with Rabaul (East New Britain) as colonial capital.
1886	October: Germany includes parts of the Solomon Islands chain north of a line of demarcation in German New Guinea, including Buka, Bougainville, Choiseual, Ysabel, Shortlands, and Ontong Java Atoll.
1893	Great Britain declares protectorate over non-German southern Solomon Islands, which become known as the British Solomon Islands Protectorate (BSIP).

1. In particular, see Regan and Griffin, *Bougainville before the Conflict*, 475–86; Carl and Garasu, *Weaving Consensus*, 94–102; Minorities at Risk Project, "Chronology for Bougainvilleans in Papua New Guinea," www.unhcr.org/refworld/docid/469f38ca17.html (accessed April 5, 2010); Bougainville Copper Ltd, "Chronology of Events," www.bougainvillecopper.com.pg/events.htm (accessed April 5, 2010), and "Chronology of Peace Process," www.bougainvillecopper.com.pg/events2.htm (accessed April 5, 2010).

1899	Line of demarcation between German New Guinea and BSIP changed so that Shortlands, Choiseul, Ysable, and Ontong Java atoll all become part of BSIP, while Bougainville and Buka remain part of German New Guinea.
1901–2	Catholic mission station established near Kieta, Bougainville.
1905	German administration post established at Kieta.
1914	September: German rule in New Guinea ends when Australian military forces take over in Rabaul. December: Australian forces occupy Kieta.
1921	May: Australia granted "C" class mandate over former German New Guinea by League of Nations, and Australia's colonial headquarters is in Rabaul.
	Australian administration establishes Bougainville district headquarters at Kieta, with subdistrict headquarters at Sohano Island in Buka Passage, between Bougainville and Buka Islands, and at Kangu on the coast near Buin.
1941	December: Japan declares war on the United States of America.
1942	January: Rabaul occupied by Japanese military. March: Japanese military occupation of Bougainville begins.
1943	August: U.S. forces land on Guadalcanal, Solomon Islands. November: U.S. forces land at Torokina, on the west coast of Bougainville, establishing huge military base (65,000 personnel).
1944	October–December: Australian forces take over Torokina military base.
1945	August 15: Japan surrenders.
1946	March: United Nations agrees to Australian trusteeship of the former League of Nations Mandated Territory of New Guinea, including Bougainville. Sohano Island in Buka Passage, becomes colonial district headquarters for Bougainville.
	Australian military forces depart Torokina. Large amounts of weapons, ammunition, bombs, and other war materials left around the extensive area of the former WWII base.
1963	Conzinc Riotinto Australia Ltd (CRA) granted authority to prospect over an area of Bougainville, including Panguna.
1964	CRA exploration geologist first walks into Panguna Valley to begin exploration.
1965	CRA begins drilling to determine size of copper and gold ore body.
1967	Mining agreement signed between Australian colonial administration and CRA, involving Bougainville Mining Ltd.
	Colonial administration district headquarters moved from Sohano (Buka Passage) to Kieta in Central Bougainville in order to be close to the Panguna mine.
1972	April: Bougainville Mining Ltd begins commercial production at the Panguna copper and gold mine.
1973	Bougainville Mining Ltd changes name to Bougainville Copper Ltd (BCL).

1975 September 1: Unilateral Declaration of Independence of Bougainville from PNG announced.
December 16: PNG's independence from Australia proclaimed.

1976 August: The Bougainville Agreement is signed between PNG and Bougainville, ending Bougainville's secession bid and agreeing on amendments to the PNG constitution to provide for a system of provincial governments with a degree of autonomy.

North Solomons Provincial Government (NSPG) established.

PNG parliament authorizes amendments to the PNG constitution to implement the Bougainville Agreement, providing for a constitutionally guaranteed system of provincial governments.

1977 PNG parliament authorizes the Organic Law on Provincial Government, providing the details of the provincial government system implementing the Bougainville Agreement.

1978 Pangua Landowners Association established.

1987 Intergenerational disputes among Panguna landowners result in the New Panguna Landowners Association. Tensions increase between landowners and BCL.

1988 New Panguna Landowners Association leaders demand K10 billion compensation from BCL, and Francis Ona (from Guava Village, within the Panguna mine-lease area) emerges as main spokesperson.

November: Bougainvillean mine workers steal explosives and blow up power line pylons supplying power to the Panguna mine.

December: BCL mining operations halted for several periods by destruction of power line pylons. PNG police mobile squads deployed to Bougainville from elsewhere in PNG. Raids by police mobile squads in Panguna area spark claims of police brutality.

1989 January–February: Increasing destruction of BCL property and attacks by armed Bougainvilleans (initially known as "militants" or "Rambos," and by early 1989 as the Bougainville Revolutionary Army, or BRA) on PNG police. PNG government under Prime Minister Rabbie Namaliu favors a negotiated settlement, establishing the Special Committee on the Crisis in the North Solomons Province, chaired by John Kaputin, MP, to investigate peaceful approaches to solving the conflict, but police appear intent on treating the situation as solely involving law and order problems.

February: Ona agrees with request of leaders from various areas of Bougainville to make Bougainville secession the main goal of the uprising

April: PNGDF deployed to Bougainville to support PNG police.

May: Repeated acts of sabotage of BCL property and attacks on buses carrying BCL personnel result in closure of Pangua mine.

June–December: Series of peace initiatives by PNG government strongly supported by Prime Minister Namaliu. NSPG and local groups fail to solve or reduce conflict, levels of violence escalate, large numbers of village houses burned by security forces, several thousand people in central Bougainville displaced from home areas and housed in government-established "care centers."

1990	January–February: Major PNGDF offensive against armed Bougainvilleans fails.
	February: BCL withdraws non-Bougainvillean workforce from Bougainville, and many other non-Bougainvilleans also depart.
	March: Ceasefire between PNG forces and BRA. PNG forces withdraw from Bougainville.
	March–May: Chaotic situation begins to develop in Bougainville, with Ona and other leaders of BRA unable to impose discipline on localized BRA elements.
	May 2: PNG imposes sea and air blockade of Bougainville.
	May 17: Francis Ona makes a Unilateral Declaration of Independence (UDI) of Bougainville from PNG.
	Bougainville Interim Government (BIG) established as civilian government in association with BRA.
	June: PNG government suspends the North Solomons Provincial Government.
	July: Talks among PNG and BIG and BRA leaders on New Zealand naval vessel, HMNZ *Endeavour*, resulting in Endeavour Accord.
	June–July: Localized armed opposition to BRA elements emerges in some areas of both Buka and Bougainville.
	September: Chiefs and other leaders from Haku, Buka, request return of PNG forces to Buka.
	September: PNG forces make forced landing in Buka Town.
	October–November: Armed opponents of BRA in Buka form the Buka Liberation Front, and numerous armed clashes occur between BLF and BRA as well as between PNGDF and BRA elements.
1991	January: Honiara Declaration signed between BRA/BIG and PNG providing for restoration of government services, but it is repudiated by BRA/BIG leaders almost immediately.
	PNG forces return to various parts of Bougainville, usually at the request of local leaders.
	In areas where conflict escalates, village people are encouraged to move to care centers, guarded by PNGDF and armed Bougainvillean groups—usually former BRA elements now opposing BRA in localized conflict.
1992	PNG forces continue to return to various parts of Bougainville, usually at the request of local leaders.
	Rabbie Namaliu replaced as prime minister by Paias Wingti following general election for PNG parliament. Wingti favors more aggressive approach against the BRA, and late in the year the PNGDF makes a forced landing near Arawa and moves to recapture the town.
	Localized armed opponents of the BRA begin to develop links and establish Bougainville Resistance Forces (BRF).

1993 February: PNGDF recaptures Arawa Town.

Conflict continues, with PNG forces returning to various areas, achieving a degree of control over perhaps one-third of Bougainville. Increasing numbers of people voluntarily move to, or are forced to move to, care centers.

1994 August: Sir Julius Chan replaces Paias Wingti as PNG prime minister, and Chan initiates contact with BRA/BIG leadership.

October: Peace conference held at Arawa, Bougainville, with security provided by regional force (SPPKF), and when most BIG/BRA fail to attend, Theodore Miriung emerges as a moderate leader.

1995 April: New provincial government established, the Bougainville Transitional Government (BTG), with Theodore Miriung elected premier.

September: BTG leaders meet with BRA/BIG representatives in Cairns.

December: Second round of talks (BTG with BRA/BIG) held in Cairns.

1996 January: PNGDF elements ambush BRA/BIG leaders returning from Cairns talks, precipitating major offensive by BRA against PNGDF; later in the year the PNGDF responds with its own major counteroffensive (Operation High-speed II), which soon founders.

September: Massacre of 11 PNG personnel at Kangu in south Bougainville.

October: Assassination of Theodore Miriung, BTG premier, widely believed to be at the hands of PNGDF and BRF elements.

November–December: Negotiations by PNG government with Sandline in order to supply mercenaries to assist the PNGDF in defeating the BRA and capturing the Panguna mine.

1997 January: PNG signs contract with Sandline.

February: Sandline mercenaries and equipment begin arriving in PNG, gradually causing controversy in PNG and the region.

March: Elements of the PNGDF arrest and then expel Sandline personnel and precipitate a national political crisis, with Prime Minister Chan forced to stand down while a commission of inquiry investigates the Sandline affair.

May: PNG cabinet approves a Bougainville peace strategy developed under the direction of Bougainville Affairs Minister Peter Barter, that emphasizes the need for a negotiated peace in Bougainville.

May–July: Bougainville leaders explore possibilities of resuming the talks they had held in Cairns late in 1995, and New Zealand government supports Barter's plan and works with Bougainville leaders to arrange for such talks to be held in New Zealand.

July: Talks between Bougainville factions and other Bougainville leaders at Burnham Barracks, New Zealand, results in Burnham Declaration.

July: Bill Skate becomes prime minister of PNG following general elections and (reflecting his support for a political settlement to the Bougainville conflict) appoints former BTG member and BRF Chairman, Sam Akoitai, as minister for Bougainville Affairs.

September: Francis Ona increasingly skeptical of emerging peace process, despite pressure from majority of BRA and BIG leaders to support the process.

October: Talks at Burnham barracks between Bougainville factions and PNG officials, result in Burnham Truce.

October–November: New Zealand and Australian governments consult Bougainville and PNG leaders about establishing New Zealand-led unarmed Truce Monitoring Group (TMG), which begins deploying to Bougainville late November.

December: New Zealand, Australia, Fiji, Vanuatu, and PNG sign multilateral agreement on mandate and formal arrangements for the TMG.

1998 January: PNG and Bougainville political leaders meet at Lincoln University, New Zealand, and sign Lincoln Agreement, which provides a broad road map for the emerging peace process.

March: Preparatory talks on ceasefire and other aspects of implementing the Lincoln Agreement held in Canberra.

April: Agreement on the implementation of the ceasefire signed.

April: Francis Ona announces Republic of Me'ekamui, which, he says, is independent under the UDI for Bougainville of May 1990.

May: Australia-led Peace Monitoring Group (PMG) replaces TMG.

July: Noah Musingku's U-Vistract Ponzi scheme begins operating in Port Moresby.

August: United Nations Political Office Bougainville (UNPOB), known in PNG (including Bougainville) as United Nations Observer Mission Bougainville (UNOMB), established following a formal request to the UN from PNG in implementation of the Lincoln Agreement.

August–November: Discussions amongst Bougainville leaders and PNG minister for Bougainville Affairs negotiate arrangements for establishing a broadly representative Bougainville Reconciliation Government, in the implementation of the Lincoln Agreement;

December: Legislation required for establishing Bougainville Reconciliation Government fails to pass in PNG parliament, and ad hoc arrangements involving formal suspension of a new provincial government for Bougainville are agreed upon for use in establishing the Bougainville Reconciliation Government. Those arrangements are opposed by John Momis (Bougainville regional member in the PNG parliament), who would have become governor of the new provincial government if it were not suspended, and various Bougainville leaders supporting continued integration of Bougainville into PNG.

1999 May: Bougainville People's Congress (BPC) established as Bougainville Reconciliation Government, with Joseph Kabui (Ona's former deputy president in the BIG) elected as president.

June: Joint Bougainville negotiating position agreed upon by BPC with senior BRA commanders, and first talks held (June 30) between Bougainville leaders and PNG on the future political status of Bougainville.

July: Bill Skate replaced by Mekere Morauta as prime minister of PNG, and Morauta indicates strong support for continuing the Bougainville peace process.

November: Legal challenge to suspension of the new provincial government mounted by John Momis succeeds.

December: Second negotiation between Bougainville and PNG on political future of Bougainville.

Momis and Kabui reach agreement on government arrangement whereby the Bougainville Interim Provincial Government (BIPG) will make decisions in consultation with the BPC.

2000 March: Negotiations on political future of Bougainville.

April: Liquidation proceedings launched in PNG courts against Noah Musingku's U-Vistract (a Ponzi scheme).

May–June: Further negotiations on political future of Bougainville.

September-October: Negotiations continue.

November: Political negotiations seem deadlocked on Bougainville demand for a constitutionally guaranteed referendum on independence for Bougainville from PNG.

December: Alexander Downer (Australian minister for foreign affairs and trade) proposes a compromise on the referendum issue involving deferral and a nonbinding outcome.

2001 January: PNG and Bougainville delegations sign an agreement on the referendum arrangements.

February: BRA and BRF leaders meet in Townsville to discuss weapons disposal.

May: BRA and BRF negotiate weapons disposal arrangements that are subsequently agreed on with PNG and incorporated into the emerging draft Bougainville Peace Agreement.

June: Draft peace agreement initialed.

August 30: Bougainville Peace Agreement signed.

September: PNG draftspersons begin preparing constitutional laws needed to implement the peace agreement, working in consultation with a joint PNG/Bougainville technical team.

October: Bougainville Peace Agreement tabled in PNG parliament.

November: Draft amendments to the PNG constitution and a draft Organic Law on Peace-Building in Bougainville prepared to implement the Bougainville Peace Agreement approved by PNG cabinet and published in the PNG *National Gazette.*

December: Weapons disposal begins with a ceremony at Torokina, where first weapons are secured by former BRA elements in containers provided by the PMG under UN mission supervision.

PNGDF elements begin withdrawal from Bougainville.

2002 January: PNG parliament votes in favor of constitutional amendments, etc., in a first vote.

March: PNG parliament votes in favor of constitutional amendments, etc., a second time.

May: Australian government established Bougainville Ex-combatants Trust Account to fund projects intended to assist former combatants from areas where weapons disposal has occurred to reintegrate them into their communities, but it is perceived as, in part, a weapons buy-back scheme.

August: Prime Minister Morauta announces approval of legal arrangements for granting of amnesty and pardon in relation to criminal offenses committed in relation to the Bougainville conflict previously negotiated between PNG and Bougainville technical teams.

Noah Musingku flees arrest for contempt of court in relation to liquidation proceedings against U-Vistract and joins Francis Ona in Guava Village in the "no-go-zone" in central Bougainville.

September: Bougainville Constitutional Commission begins work on developing a constitution for the Autonomous Bougainville Government.

October–December: Bougainville Constitutional Commission conducts extensive public consultation on a new constitution for Bougainville.

October–November: After weapons containment has continued throughout the year in many areas, several containers are broken into and weapons removed.

2003 February: First draft of Bougainville Constitution released by Bougainville Constitutional Commission for public consultation.

February–March: Further rounds of public consultation on the draft constitution conducted by the Bougainville Constitutional Commission.

March: Second draft of Bougainville Constitution released for public consultation.

April: Last elements of PNGDF depart Bougainville.

June: Australian Minister for Foreign Affairs and Trade Alexander Downer announces decision to deploy Bougainville Transitional Team (BTT) from July 2003, after PMG ceases to operate June 30.

July: BTT installed.

July 25: UNOMB Director Noel Sinclair announces verification of completion of stage 2 of the weapons disposal process contained in the Bougainville Peace Agreement.

August 7: As a result of the verification of completion of stage 2 of weapons disposal, the amendments to the PNG Constitution and the Organic Law on Peace-Building in Bougainville come into effect, as formally proclaimed by notice in the PNG *National Gazette*.

December: PNG cabinet formally delegates to the Bougainville Interim Provincial Government some authority over the police serving in Bougainville.

BRA and BRF leaders formally agree that the method of final disposal of the contained weapons should be by destroying the weapons, and formal agreement is reached with PNG on the subject a few days later.

December 31: BTT ceases to operate.

2004 January: UNPOB formally changes name to UNOMB.

February: PNG government officials formally consult with the Bougainville Constitutional Commission about the contents of the draft Bougainville Constitution, and some differences emerge.

February 29: Noel Sinclair departs PNG and is replaced as director of UNOMB by Thor Stenbock.

April: PNG government announces establishment of ministerial committee on Bougainville matters.

May: Meeting of Bougainville Constitutional Commission representatives with the PNG ministerial committee resolves most difficulties about the draft Bougainville Constitution.

May: Coronation of Francis Ona and Noah Musingku and announcement of "twin kingdoms agreement."

July: Bougainville Constitutional Commission finalizes report and draft constitution.

September: Jeffrey Richards and Rex James Nesbitt join Ona and Musingku at Guava, their roles never being clearly understood.

September–November: Bougainville Constituent Assembly debates draft constitution and report of the Bougainville Constitutional Commission, and PNG and Bougainville officials consult to resolve final concerns about the draft before the Bougainville Constituent Assembly formally adopts the constitution.

December: PNG cabinet endorses the Bougainville Constitution.

AusAID establishes Governance and Implementation Fund (GIF) to support implementation of autonomy and provides incentives for adoption by the ABG of good financial management and planning standard.

Noah Musingku has a "falling out" with Francis Ona and departs Guava Village for his home area of Tonu (Siwai). In the meantime, Ona has dismissed or suspended several senior advisers, who base themselves in the area of the former BCL headquarters at Panguna, a few kilometres from Ona's home base at Guava Village.

2005	January–April: Preparations begin for electing and establishing the Autonomous Bougainville Government; Ona speaks at public meetings in Arawa, Buka, and Buin.
	April–June: First general election for the ABG, with Joseph Kabui elected president.
	May: UNOMB director announces completion of stage 3 (disposal by destruction) of the weapons disposal process.
	June 15: Formal inauguration of the ABG.
	June 30: UNOMB ceases to operate.
	July: Francis Ona dies.
	October 2005: Five former Fiji Army commandos join Musingku at Tonu, raising fears that Musingku is contemplating a coup against the ABG.
	Late 2005: Localized armed conflict develops in south Bougainville.
2006	March: Richards and Nesbitt leave Guava and are arrested in Buka, but they are subsequently released by police authorities in Port Moresby.
	November: ABG makes first formal request to the PNG government for transfer of powers and functions, including those in relation to mining, oil, and gas.
	November 26: Former BRA and BRF elements, operating under the name “Bougainville Freedom Fighters,” attack Musingku’s headquarters at Tonu; one of the attackers killed in the ensuing armed clash.
	Localized armed conflict in south Bougainville continues sporadically throughout the year.
2007	February: Four of the five Fijian former commandos leave Musingku and are charged with various criminal offenses; they are held in police cells in Buka, where they remain for over a year.
	August: Panguna Communiqué signed between ABG and Me’ekamui Government of Unity (MGU) leaders.
	Localized armed conflict in south Bougainville continues sporadically throughout the year.
2008	January: Agreement reached in Joint Supervisory Body (JSB) on a staged process for transfer to the ABG of mining, oil, and gas functions and powers.
	March: ABG and PNG, meeting in the JSB, sign a memorandum of understanding on implementing the first stages for transferring mining, oil, and gas functions and powers.
	June: Death of Joseph Kabui, first president of the ABG.
	December: By-election for president’s seat, with James Tanis elected second president of Bougainville.
	Localized armed conflict in south Bougainville continues sporadically throughout the year.

District office established at Panguna, and basic services begin to be restored in the "no-go-zone."

2009 January: James Tanis sworn in as president of the ABG.

February: ABG requests transfer of numerous additional functions and powers from the PNG government.

June: Team from U.S. State Department Office of Weapons Removal and Abatement visits Torokina, on the west coast of Bougainville, to examine weapons and other items left at the U.S. and Australian military base there.

July: Noah Musingku, of U-Vistract, announces he is issuing his own currency with which he intends to repay investors in his Ponzi scheme.

September: Contractors engaged by U.S. State Department Office of Weapons Removal and Abatement visit Torokina and in one week identify 148 sites with weapons, bombs, and other materiel.

December: PNG announces agreement to transfer five new functions and powers (time zones, women's affairs, and others)

Efforts by community leaders, ABG, and others contribute to ending of localized armed conflict in south Bougainville.

2010 January–March: Former Bougainville governor and potential candidate in ABG elections, John Momis, has several meetings with a leader of one of the groups involved in localized conflict in south Bougainville, encouraging him to join the peace process and support the ABG elections.

March 17: Memorandum of understanding signed between ABG, MGU, and original Me'ekamui government.

March 26: Writs issued for second general election for the ABG.

March–April: Contractors engaged by U.S. State Department Office of Weapons Removal and Abatement in PNG preparing for three-month clean-up operation at Torokina, expected to begin late in April.

April 2: Period for nomination of candidates for the second ABG general election closed.

Index

About the Author

Anthony J. Regan has worked in Bougainville, Papua New Guinea, since 1981. He lived there from 1981 to 1991, 1994–97, and 2002–04. He was an adviser to all of the Bougainville parties in the Bougainville peace process and during the negotiation and implementation of the Bougainville Peace Agreement, signed in August 2001, including development of the constitution for the Autonomous Bougainville Government under the agreement. He was a full-time adviser during Uganda's postconflict constitution-making process for three years, 1991–94, where he advised the Ugandan government bodies responsible for the development of a new constitution. He continues to advise the Bougainville government on constitutional matters. He has also had limited involvement in either conflict resolution or postconflict constitutional development work in relation to Solomon Islands, Timor Leste, Sri Lanka, and Nagaland (India).

Jennings Randolph Program for International Peace

This book is a fine example of the work produced by senior fellows in the Jennings Randolph fellowship program of the United States Institute of Peace. As part of the statute establishing the Institute, Congress envisioned a program that would appoint "scholars and leaders of peace from the United States and abroad to pursue scholarly inquiry and other appropriate forms of communication on international peace and conflict resolution." The program was named after Senator Jennings Randolph of West Virginia, whose efforts over four decades helped to establish the Institute.

Since 1987, the Jennings Randolph Program has played a key role in the Institute's effort to build a national center of research, dialogue, and education on critical problems of conflict and peace. Fellows come from a wide variety of academic and other professional backgrounds. They conduct research at the Institute and participate in the Institute's outreach activities to policy makers, the academic community, and the American public.

Each year approximately twelve senior fellows are in residence at the Institute. Fellowship recipients are selected by the Institute's board of directors in a competitive process. For further information on the program, please contact the program staff at (202) 457-1700, or visit our Web site at www.usip.org.

United States Institute of Peace Press

Since 1991, the United States Institute of Peace Press has published over 150 books on the prevention, management, and peaceful resolution of international conflicts—among them such venerable titles as Raymond Cohen's *Negotiating Across Cultures*; *Leashing the Dogs of War*, edited by Chester A. Crocker, Fen Osler Hampson, and Pamela Aall; I. William Zartman's *Peacemaking and International Conflict*; and *American Negotiating Behavior*, by Richard H. Solomon and Nigel Quinney. All our books arise from research and fieldwork sponsored by the Institute's many programs. In keeping with the best traditions of scholarly publishing, each volume undergoes both thorough internal review and blind peer review by external subject experts to ensure that the research, scholarship, and conclusions are balanced, relevant, and sound. As the Institute prepares to move to its new headquarters on the National Mall in Washington, D.C., the Press is committed to extending the reach of the Institute's work by continuing to publish significant and sustainable works for practitioners, scholars, diplomats, and students.

Valerie Norville
Director

United States Institute of Peace

The United States Institute of Peace is an independent, nonpartisan institution established and funded by Congress. The Institute provides analysis, training, and tools to help prevent, manage, and end violent international conflicts, promote stability, and professionalize the field of peacebuilding.